EXPLRING

SPANISH

Second Edition Revised

Joan G. Sheeran
J. Patrick McCarthy

Consultants
James F. Funston
Alejandro Vargas Bonilla

EMC/Paradigm Publishing, Saint Paul, Minnesota

Illustrator:
Jackie Urbanovic

Cover Design:
Jennifer Wreisner

Photo Credits:
Brett, Robert J.: viii (tl), ix (br)
Consejo de Promoción Turística de México, S.A. en
*   Chicago: 97*
Fried, Robert: iii (all), vi (t), vii (all), viii (bl), ix (tr, bl),
*   xi (cr, cl), xii (b)*
Funston, James F.: ix (tl)
Kraft, Wolfgang S.: viii (tr, c, br), x (tl)
Mike Woodside Photography: cover photos
NASA: Earth
Secretaría de Turismo de Argentina: vi (b)
Simson, David: x (tr, bl), xi (t, b), xii (tr)
Tourist Office of Spain: vi (c), x (br), xii (tl), 70

ISBN 0-8219-2404-4

Published by EMC/Paradigm Publishing
875 Montreal Way
St. Paul, Minnesota 55102
800-328-1452
www.emcp.com
E-mail: educate@emcp.com

Printed in the United States of America
    2 3 4 5 6 7 8 9 10 XXX 07 06 05 04 03 02

INTRODUCTION

¡Hola y bienvenidos!

Hello and welcome! You are about to explore a world where hundreds of millions of people communicate in Spanish every day. For example, did you know that over 30 million people in the United States speak Spanish on a daily basis? Did you also know that Spanish is an official language of the Commonwealth of Puerto Rico? In addition, Spanish is the official language of 18 Latin American countries, the African nation of

Equatorial Guinea, and, of course, Spain. Because you probably will find yourself having to speak Spanish at one point or another in your lifetime, you are going to learn some common words and expressions in *Exploring Spanish* that are used often by native Spanish speakers. Then you will be able to understand some of the things they say, and they will be able to understand you.

If you practice correct pronunciation with your teacher or with the recordings, you will learn to speak Spanish even better. Besides being able to understand and speak basic Spanish, you will find out some information about countries where Spanish is spoken and get some insight into their rich traditions in art, music, and literature.

Hopefully, throughout your journey you will discover that learning Spanish is fun and not too difficult. Be sure to practice your Spanish at every opportunity both in and outside of class. As with any other skill, the more you practice, the better you will become.

As the world continues to shrink and as countries and people grow closer and closer together, it is important to be able to communicate with each other. So, let's get started! *¡Vamos!*

Table of Contents

Exploring

...countries and cities

México

Argentina

La Alhambra, España

San Juan, Puerto Rico

Machu Picchu, Perú

...language

Cancún, México

Lima, Perú

Chapultepec México

Ciudad de México, México

El Bosque Encantado

*Comida Criolla
(Todo Hecho al Momento)
*Tacos de:
Pollo
Carne
Jueyes
Langosta
Camarones
Y Mucho Más...
*Alcapurrias
*Bacalaitos
*Piononos
*Rellenos

Batidas Piña Colada,
Jugos Naturales, y Más.

El Yunque, Puerto Rico

San Juan, Puerto Rico

ESTACIONAMIENTO RESERVADO
$ 250.00 MULTA

Guayaquil, Ecuador

Quito, Ecuador

...daily life

Santo Domingo, República Dominicana

Madrid, España

Barcelona, España

San Salvador, El Salvador

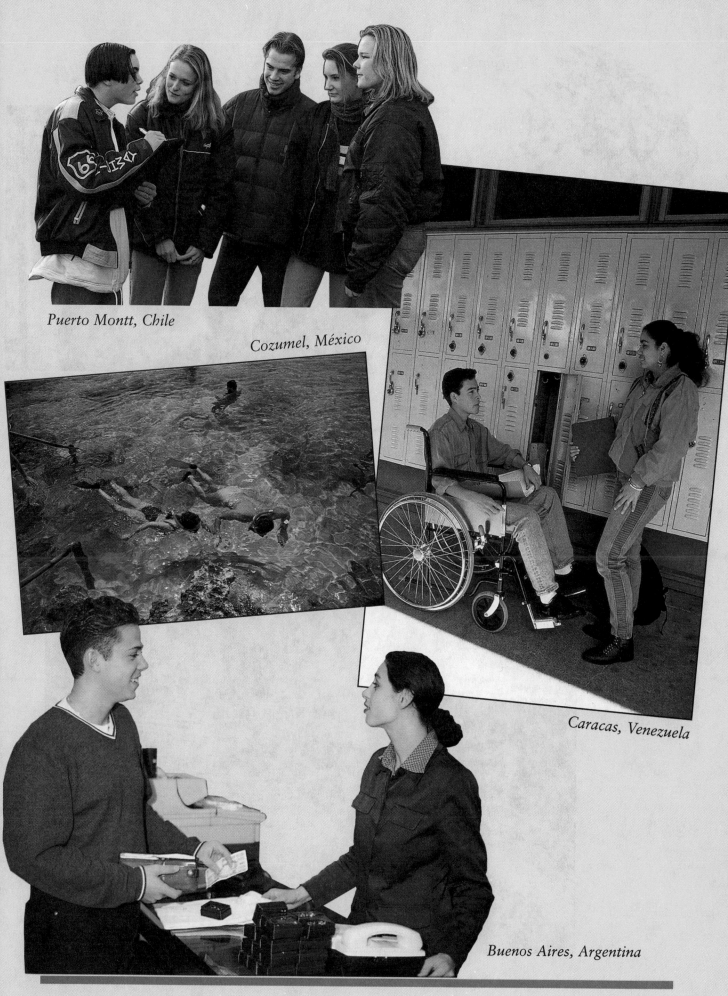

Puerto Montt, Chile

Cozumel, México

Caracas, Venezuela

Buenos Aires, Argentina

España

...and culture.

Puerto Rico

Puerto Rico

GREETINGS AND EXPRESSIONS OF COURTESY
Saludos y expresiones de cortesía

Buenos días.
Good morning.
Buenas tardes.
Good afternoon.
Buenas noches.
Good night.

Expresiones de cortesía

Por favor. —— Please.
Gracias. —— Thank you.
De nada. —— You're welcome.
Perdón. —— Excuse me.
Lo siento —— I'm sorry.

Hola. —— Hello. Hi.
Adiós. —— Good-bye.
Hasta luego. — See you later.
Hasta mañana. – See you tomorrow.

Sí.   ¡No!

Buena suerte.

GOOD LUCK.

¿Cómo te llamas?
What's your name?

Me llamo Pedro.
My name is Pedro.

Hablas español, ¿no?
You speak Spanish, don't you?

Sí, hablo español.
Yes, I speak Spanish.

Encantado.
I'm delighted to meet you.

¿Cómo estás?
How are you?

Bien, gracias.
¿Y tú?
Fine, thanks. And you?

Así, así.
So-so.

¿Hablas español?
Do you speak Spanish?

No, no hablo español.
No, I don't speak Spanish.

Mucho gusto. – I'm pleased to meet you.   alemán (German),
francés (French), inglés (English), italiano (Italian), ruso (Russian).

La cortesía mucho vale y poco cuesta.
Politeness is worth a lot and costs little.

Me llamo:

Amanda	Adán
Cándida	Alberto
Dolores	Andrés
Evita	Carlos
Francisca	Daniel
Guadalupe	David
Isabel	Felipe
Juanita	Francisco
Lucía	Guillermo
Luz	Jaime
Marisela	José
Mónica	Juan Carlos
Paloma	Lorenzo
Patricia	Luis
Pilar	Marcos
Raquel	Mateo
Rosario	Miguel
Sara	Patricio
Susana	Ramón
Yolanda	Tomás

Exercises

A Escoge la palabra que no pertenece. *Choose the word that doesn't fit.*

1. Hola.   Por favor.   De nada.   Gracias.
2. Adiós.   Buenas tardes.   Hasta luego.   Hasta mañana.
3. ¿Hablas alemán?   ¿Cómo estás?   Así, así.   Bien, gracias.
4. Buenas tardes.   Encantado.   Buenos días.   Buenas noches.
5. inglés   francés   alemán   De nada.

B Escoge los nombres de las chicas. *Choose the girls' names.*

1. Cándida
2. Miguel
3. Adán
4. Luz
5. Carlos
6. Yolanda
7. José
8. Sara
9. Evita
10. Alberto

C Contesta en español. Escribe tus respuestas. *Answer the questions in Spanish. Write your answers.*

1. ¿Hablas español? _____

2. ¿Cómo te llamas? _____

3. ¿Cómo estás? _____

D Escribe al lado del dibujo la expresión española que pertenece. *Write next to each picture the Spanish expression that fits.*

1. _____

2. _____

¿Cómo estás?
Hola.
Me llamo...
Gracias.
Por favor.

3. _____

4. _____

5. _____

6. _____

7. _____

4

E Short answers. (En español, por favor.)

1. How do you greet someone in the morning?

   _____.

2. How do you greet someone in the evening?

   _____.

3. Two expressions at an introduction are:

   _____.

4. How do you wish someone "good luck"?

   _____.

5. Finish this sentence:

   Hablo _____.

6. "¡Hola!" is used when addressing: (a) Paco   (b) el señor González

   _____.

7. Spanish speakers sometimes shake hands to greet each other or to say good-bye. (a) Sí. (b) No.

   _____.

8. Answer this question: "¿Cómo te llamas?"

   _____.

9. "Good-bye" means

   _____.

10. "Sí" is the opposite of

   _____.

F Contesta en español. Escribe tus respuestas. *Answer in Spanish. Write your answers.*

1. Evita: Hola. Me llamo Evita. ¿Y tú?

   Adán: _____.

2. Juan Carlos: Buenos días, Francisca. ¿Cómo estás?

   Francisca: _____.

3. Juanita: ¿Hablas español?

   Patricio: Sí, _____.

Crucigrama

G

Vertical

1. "...tardes."
2. I'm sorry.
4. Hi!
5. "Por favor."
9. "Good-bye."
10. "Me...Juanita."
12. "Mucho...."
14. "¿Y...?"
16. opposite of "no"

Horizontal

3. "...días."
6. "¿...estás?"
7. "Buenos...."
8. María says, "..."
   when she meets José.
11. "Hasta...."
13. "Buena...."
15. "¿Cómo...?"
17. courtesy

LA CLAVE

Es una publicación de
EMPRESA DE COMUNICACIONES LA CLAVE S.A.
Calle 70A Nº 13-45
Teléfonos: 2496843 - 2104841
Apartado Aéreo 089109
Bogotá, Colombia

Consejo Editorial: Ramón Jimeno, Emilio Juan Ruiz, Cecilia López M., José María Domenech, Germán Fernández, Germán Gélvez, Mario Méndez

Presidente: Emilio Juan Ruiz

Editor: Germán Gélvez

Jefe de Redacción: Mario Méndez

Editor Gráfico: Alfonso Durier
Nacional: César Aguirre, Alvaro Duque
Internacional: Juan Carlos Ruiz
Economía: Roberto Sol
Investigación: Richard Agudelo, Leticia Plata
Política: Omar Roberto Rodríguez
Deportes: Juan Carlos Castillo
Cultura: Adonay Ariza
Sociedad: Margarita Márquez
Farándula: Fernando Motta

Corrección: Enrique Castañeda

Caricaturista: Rubens

Corresponsales:
Omar Nieto, Jaime Seguí Font

Columnistas: Cecilia López, Ramón Jimeno, Arturo Uslar Pietri, Luis Bernardo Flórez, Mauricio Restrepo, Eduardo Lora

Colaboradores: Guillermo Hoyos, Gustavo Gómez, Jairo Morales

Servicios de Prensa: Efe, Prensa Verde

Jefe de Producción: Esmeralda Akle

Director de Arte: Edison Blanco P.

Fotomecánica: SoftPage Ltda.
Impresión: Tecimpre S.A.
Distribución: Distribuidoras Unidas

Presidente Junta Directiva: Cecilia López M.
Gerente General: Humberto Pérez Díaz
Gerente Comercial: Cristina Gutiérrez
Relaciones Públicas: Consuelo Martínez
Director de Suscripciones: Henry González
Circulación: Enrique Rodríguez, Luis Fernando Moreno
Asistente de Dirección:
Cielo Patricia Artunduaga

Resolución Min-Gobierno
Nº 276 de 02-04-93 - Permiso de Tarifa Postal
Reducida Nº 1331-Adpostal - ISSN 0121-7399

PUERTO RICO ¡BienVenidos!

David
Del hebreo Dawidh, significa "amado". El primer portador conocido de este nombre fue el segundo hijo del rey de Israel.

Laura
Proviene del latín laurus, y significa "coronado de laurel", aludiendo a Apolo, ya que sus templos se adornaban con esta planta.

Pregúntale a tu amigo Sebastián

PESCADOS Y MARISCOS ANTONIO
PLAZA 19 DE OCTUBRE
MERCADILLO DEL FONTAN - PUESTO 18
TEL. 521 55 79 - OVIEDO

Tarjeta Conavi
RED MULTICOLOR
004 258 221
JUAN RODRÍGUEZ

CLASSROOM OBJECTS
Objetos de la clase

¿Qué es esto?
Es un...
Es una...

What's this?
It's a....

un mapa — a map

una pared — a wall

una clase — a classroom, class

una ventana — a window

un reloj — a clock

un cuadro

una punta — a point

un lápiz — a pencil

una goma — an eraser

un sacapuntas — a pencil sharpener

una bandera — a flag

una pizarra — a board

a picture

una silla — a chair

un borrador — an eraser

una tiza — a chalk

un escritorio — a desk

un estante de libros — a bookcase

un libro — a book

un papel — a paper

un cuaderno — a notebook

una papelera — a wastebasket

un bolígrafo — a ballpoint pen

una regla — a ruler

un pupitre — a desk

"Boli" is the short form of "bolígrafo."

Es mejor evitar que remediar. An ounce of prevention is worth a pound of cure.

Exercises

A **Listening Comprehension**

Your teacher will point out twenty-four classroom objects. As he or she pronounces the name of each in Spanish, find it on the list below and place the appropriate number after it.

una bandera _____   un estante de libros _____

un libro _____   una clase _____

una tiza _____   un escritorio _____

un cuaderno _____   una papelera _____

un bolígrafo _____   una silla _____

un lápiz _____   una goma _____

una pizarra _____   una pared _____

un borrador _____   un papel _____

un mapa _____   una punta _____

una regla _____   una ventana _____

un cuadro _____   un sacapuntas _____

un pupitre _____   un reloj _____

B Answer each question in English.

1. Where in the classroom is the "bandera"?

_____

2. What is indicated by the "reloj"?

_____

3. What is hung on a "pared" to decorate a room?

_____

C Escoge la respuesta correcta. *Choose the correct response.*

1. One writes on the "pizarra" with....
    a. chalk   b. a pencil
2. Light enters through the....
    a. silla   b. ventana
3. The (chalk)board is cleaned with a....
    a. goma   b. borrador
4. The "sacapuntas"....
    a. sharpens pencils   b. makes chalk
5. Waste materials are deposited in the....
    a. pupitre   b. papelera

D Escribe en español la palabra o frase que corresponde a cada dibujo. *Write the Spanish word or phrase that corresponds to each picture.*

1.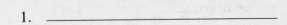

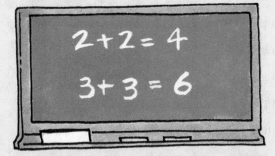

2. _____

3.

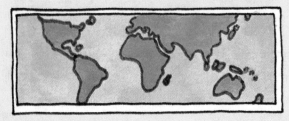

4. _____

5.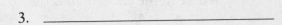

6. _____

7. _____

8. _____

9. _____

10. _____

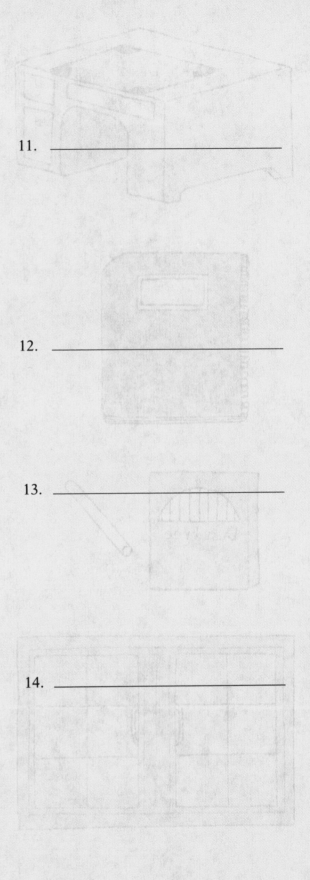

11. _____

12. _____

13. _____

14. _____

15. _____

E Completa las frases. *Fill in the missing words.*

1. ¿————————————— es esto?

2. ————————————— un bolígrafo.

3. Es ————————————— papelera.

4. Es ————————————— borrador.

F Escribe la letra que falta. *Write the missing letter.*

1. l__piz
2. cua__erno
3. __apel
4. sill__
5. es__ante de libros
6. bo__ígrafo
7. r__loj
8. __uadro

9. pape__era
10. p__pitre
11. __apa
12. v__ntana
13. pun__a
14. tiz__
15. clas__
16. borra__or

17. band__ra
18. g__ma
19. reg__a
20. __acapuntas
21. par__d
22. p__zarra
23. __scritorio
24. li__ro

Crucigrama

G

Vertical

1. written on with pen or pencil
2. makes a point
3. notebook
5. the teacher's desk
7. outline of a country
9. needs sharpening
10. garbage receptacle
11. where pupil works
12. group of students
14. cleans (chalk) boards
18. used to write on the board

Horizontal

4. window
6. male student's name: Michael
8. place to sit
10. female student's name: Pat
13. measures things
15. used with chalk
16. read by student
17. holds books ("...de libros")
19. removes errors

Blíster de 3 rotuladores
PILOT + un bolígrafo
BPS-GP de regalo,
~~875~~
595

EL DIÁLOGO ENTRE PADRES E HIJOS
Catherine Petit
8½" x 5¾" - 249 pgs.
Cód. 302 - Reg. $13.95

Libro práctico para el mejor entendimiento familiar.

74.250

Papelera metálica
~~650~~ **450**

Silla tapizada de color negro o rojo,
~~4.950~~
3.750

CLASSROOM COMMANDS
Los mandatos de la clase

Repite.
Repeat.

Contesta la pregunta.
Answer the question.

Habla.
Speak.

Dilo en español.
Say it in Spanish.

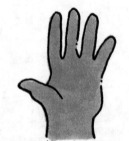

Levanta la mano.
Raise your hand.

Saca papel.
Take out paper.

Abre el libro.
Open the book.

Cierra el libro.
Close the book.

Escribe.
Write.

Escucha.
Listen.

Lee.
Read.

Siéntate.
Sit down.
Be seated.

Completa las frases.
Complete the sentences.

Pasa a la pizarra.
Go to the board.

A palabras necias, oídos sordos.

To foolish words lend a deaf ear.

Exercises

A Do what your teacher commands.

B Escribe en español, por favor. *Write in Spanish, please.*

1. (Speak.) _____

2. (Say.) _____

3. (Answer.) _____

C Do as the following command says.

Escribe <u>tu nombre completo</u>. _____
        (your complete name)

D Asocia la frase en inglés con la palabra en español. *Match the English with the Spanish.*

A		B
1. abrir _____		a. to write
2. contestar _____		b. to open
3. escribir _____		c. to speak
4. cerrar _____		d. to answer
5. hablar _____		e. to close

E Escribe un mandato en español para cada dibujo. *Write a Spanish command for each picture.*

1. _____

2. _____

3. _____

4. _____

5. _____

F Completa cada frase en español. *Complete each sentence in Spanish.*

1. _____ papel.

2. Levanta la _____.

3. _____ la pregunta.

4. Dilo en _____.

5. _____ a la pizarra.

6. Completa las _____.

7. _____ el libro.

G En cada grupo escoge el mandato correcto. *Choose the correct command in each group.*

1. Speak. (Lee.   Repite.   Habla.)
2. Answer. (Completa. Contesta. Abre.)
3. Listen. (Dilo.   Escribe.   Escucha.)
4. Write.   (Escribe.   Lee.   Escucha.)
5. Read.   (Lee   Pasa.   Saca.)

CÓMETELA A MORDISCOS

NUEVO Y DELICIOSO HELADO SUAVE DE VAINILLA CUBIERTO DE RICO CHOCOLATE CON TROCITOS DE MANÍ

Maxilatto

MAXIlatto

Lo Máximo en Helados

DE VENTA EN SUPERMERCADOS Y TIENDAS DEL PAÍS.

Si dudas, pregunta.

Ayuntamiento de Barcelona

MATENGA EL ÁREA LIMPIA GRACIAS

MAINTAIN CLEAN THE AREA THANKS

Di **NO** a las drogas.

LA VALLENATA

LA EMISORA CACHETE

¡Escucha la mejor música salsa!

CUIDADO PERROS BRAVOS

ACÉRQUESE... GENTE AMABLE

MUNDIAL SEGUROS

Lee

¡Y lo sabrás todo!

Después de todo se lo merece

¡Escápese!

USTED CUENTA CON **MEXICANA** La Primera Línea Aérea de México

NO ENTRE

EXCEPTO TAXIS

4 NUMBERS
Los números

¿Cuánto es...? How much is...?
¿Cuántos son...? How many are...?

1 uno
2 dos
3 tres
4 cuatro
5 cinco

6 seis
7 siete
8 ocho
9 nueve
10 diez

11 once
12 doce
13 trece
14 catorce
15 quince

16 dieciséis
17 diecisiete
18 dieciocho
19 diecinueve

20 veinte
21 veintiuno
22 veintidós
23 veintitrés
24 veinticuatro
25 veinticinco
26 veintiséis
27 veintisiete
28 veintiocho
29 veintinueve

30 treinta
31 treinta y uno
32 treinta y dos

40 cuarenta
41 cuarenta y uno
42 cuarenta y dos

50 cincuenta
51 cincuenta y uno
52 cincuenta y dos

60 sesenta
61 sesenta y uno
62 sesenta y dos

70 setenta
71 setenta y uno
72 setenta y dos

80 ochenta
81 ochenta y uno
82 ochenta y dos

90 noventa
91 noventa y uno
92 noventa y dos

100 cien(to)
200 doscientos
1.000 mil

Más vale pájaro en mano que ciento volando.

A bird in the hand is worth two in the bush.

20

Supplementary Vocabulary

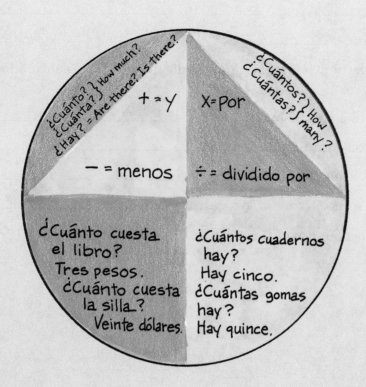

Exercises

A After you have studied the numbers and practiced saying them, try to write these numbers from memory. (En español, por favor.)

one _____   six _____

two _____   seven _____

three _____   eight _____

four _____   nine _____

five _____   ten _____

B Rate yourself. How did you do? Circle your evaluation.

1. very well   2. fairly well   3. poorly

C Practice again. Escribe los números.

EJEMPLO: ___4___

1. cinco _____   4. nueve _____

2. ocho _____   5. siete _____

3. uno _____

D Escribe en español el nombre de cada número.

3 _____   6 _____

4 _____   10 _____

2 _____

E Tell whether the following equations indicate addition, subtraction, multiplication, or division.

1. Catorce dividido por siete son dos. _____

2. Dos y diez son doce. _____

3. Ocho por tres son veinticuatro. _____

4. Diecinueve menos trece son seis. _____

F Write the numbers in Spanish again and don't look at exercise A. (En español, por favor.)

1 _____   2 _____

6 _____   9 _____

8 _____   4 _____

3 _____   7 _____

5 _____   10 _____

¿Cuántos objetos hay en cada grupo? *How many objects are there in each group?*

 = _____

 = _____

 = _____

 = _____

 = _____

H ¿Cuántos objetos hay en total? *How many objects are there altogether?* _____

Now, write this sum in Spanish. _____

I   Escribe las respuestas en español.

      EJEMPLO: $6 - 4 = $ <u> dos </u>

1. $12 \times 4 = $ _____

2. $30 - 10 = $ _____

3. $8 - 6 = $ _____

4. $12 + 18 = $ _____

5. $100 \div 2 = $ _____

6. $60 + 10 = $ _____

7. $30 - 15 = $ _____

8. $80 \div 2 = $ _____

9. $10 \times 10 = $ _____

10. $15 + 4 = $ _____

J   Your teacher will say ten numbers in Spanish. Write the corresponding numerals.

a. _____   f. _____

b. _____   g. _____

c. _____   h. _____

d. _____   i. _____

e. _____   j. _____

K   How many interior angles are there in each figure? Circle the number.

cuatro
ocho
diez
tres

cinco
tres
cuatro
siete

siete
seis
once
cinco

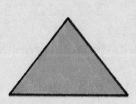

cinco
nueve
ocho
once

L Lee el párrafo.

En la clase hay muchos objetos. Hay ocho gomas, veintitrés sillas, doce cuadernos y una papelera. Una goma cuesta treinta y cinco centavos y una silla cuesta diecisiete dólares. El cuaderno cuesta un dólar, veinticinco centavos y la papelera cuesta tres dólares.

Completa las frases.

1. En la clase hay....
   - a. tres objetos
   - b. pocos objetos
   - c. mil objetos
   - d. muchos objetos

2. En total hay...objetos en la clase. (*Add.*)
   - a. 4
   - b. 44
   - c. 25
   - d. 13

Escoge la respuesta correcta.

3. ¿Cuánto cuesta una silla?
   - a. 17 dólares
   - b. 3 dólares
   - c. 90 centavos
   - d. 5 centavos

4. ¿Cuántas gomas hay en la clase?
   - a. ocho
   - b. ochenta
   - c. dieciocho
   - d. veintiocho

5. ¿Cuántas papeleras hay en la clase?
   - a. once
   - b. una
   - c. muchas
   - d. ochenta

Crucigrama

M

Vertical

1. $2 \times 3 =$
2. $4 + 4 =$
3. five dozens
5. a dozen plus one
7. Spanish for multiplication
8. how many
9. ½ century = ...years
11. $1 - 0 =$
12. five times twenty, plus one = ... *uno*

Horizontal

1. one hour and ten minutes = ...minutes
4. name of the sign indicating subtraction
5. $8 - 5 =$
6. one fewer than a dozen
9. $56 \div 4 =$
10. $50 - 10 =$
12. how much
13. $7 + 2 =$
14. the number of items in a pair
15. $70 - 40 =$
16. $80 + 8 =$

Picadillo de Tomate

TIEMPO DE PREPARACIÓN: **30** MINUTOS • RECETA PARA: **4** PORCIONES • KILOCALORÍAS POR PORCIÓN: **261**

INGREDIENTES: 2 tomates grandes maduros pelados, sin semilla y picados • 3 cucharadas de cebolla cabezona finamente picada • 1 cucharada de cilantro finamente picado • Salsa de pollo, ají, sal y pimienta al gusto • 4 tortillas de maíz.

PREPARACIÓN: Mezclar todos los ingredientes. Colocar sobre las tortillas de maíz y servir.

¡EN MINUTOS!
Deliciosos Menús

HOTELES

HOTELES EN JALISCO

HOTELES	NÚMEROS DE TELÉFONO
SAN MIGUEL EL ALTO	
Mesón de los Cristeros	825 04 Fax 821 32
SAN JUAN DE LOS LAGOS	
Balha Grande	546 06 Fax 504 18
Posada Arcos	515 80 Fax 500 09
Posada del Marqués	501 30 540 02
Primavera	515 06 Fax 522 20
Topacio	527 45 Fax 511 12
Posada Camino Real	527 15
Diana	520 09 515 58
Dorado	514 32
Francés	501 95
Hotel Coral	5 30 50
Hotel Fanny	5 43 43
Hotel Jerusalem	5 30 03
Hotel Plaza las Torres	5 21 05

CLASIFICACION ANTER.

REGIONAL PREFERENTE

Equipo	P_{tos}	J	G	E	P
1. Piloñesa	38	20	10	8	2
2. Langreo B	37	19	11	4	5
3. Andés	35	20	10	5	4
4. Europa	32	20	9	5	6
5. Covadonga	31	20	9	6	7
6. Tapia	31	20	9	4	7
7. Praviano	31	20	8	7	5
8. Trasona	31	20	8	7	5
9. Aboño	30	19	9	3	7
10. Lenense	30	19	8	6	5
11. Quintueles	27	19	6	9	4
12. Lada	27	19	7	6	6
13. Villaverde	25	20	7	4	9
14. Llanes	25	19	6	7	6
15. Valdesoto	23	19	8	6	7
16. Ceares	22	19	5	7	7
17. Juvencia	22	20	5	7	4
18. Camocha	22	20	7	4	9
19. G. Lafuerza	16	20	4	4	12
20. Treviense	12	18	3	3	12
	10	19	2	4	13

HOSPITALES

RESTAURANTES

BANCOS

HOTELES

TELÉPHONOS

RENTA DE AUTOMÓVILES

GEOGRAPHY
Geografía

5

MAR CANTABRICO

FRANCIA

LOS PIRINEOS

OCEANO
ATLANTICO

RIO EBRO

RIO DUERO

• BARCELONA

MADRID ◉

MAR MEDITERRANEO

RIO TAJO

RIO GUADIANA

RIO GUADALQUIVIR

ESPAÑA

•SEVILLA

• GRANADA

EL PORTUGAL

• MALAGA

LOS ESTADOS UNIDOS

RIO GRANDE

RIO BRAVO

OCEANO
PACIFICO

GOLFO DE MEXICO

SALTILLO •

MERIDA

MEXICO

MEXICO D.F. ◉

VERACRUZ

ACAPULCO•

Poderoso caballero es don Dinero.

Money talks.

SPAIN
Important Cities

Madrid, the capital of Spain and its most populated city, is the geographical, artistic and cultural center of the nation.

Barcelona is Spain's largest seaport and its second largest city. It is the nation's most industrial city and is more cosmopolitan than Madrid.

Málaga—Spain's third largest city and the capital of the province of Andalucía—is a major Mediterranean seaport and Spain's summer playground.

Granada, the ancient capital of the Moorish empire, is a skiing center and site of the Alhambra, the palace of the ruling Moorish calif. The burial place of King Ferdinand and Queen Isabel is located in Granada's famous Gothic cathedral.

Sevilla is located on the Guadalquivir River and is the nation's largest inland port. It was once a center of Moorish culture and is still the site of the Giralda, a marvel of Moorish architecture.

Important Rivers

The *Ebro* is the only river in Spain that flows eastward. It empties into the Mediterranean.

The *Tajo* is Spain's longest river. It flows through Toledo, passes through Portugal and empties into the Atlantic at Lisbon.

The *Guadalquivir* is the most navigable river in Spain. It flows through Sevilla, its chief commercial port, and empties into the Atlantic.

The *Duero* drains north central and northwestern Spain. It flows west through Portugal to the Atlantic.

The *Guadiana* flows west from La Mancha to the border of Portugal. It then flows south to the Mediterranean.

> With the exception of the Guadalquivir, the rivers of Spain are for the most part unnavigable. They serve as a source of electric power and are used for pleasure boating. They are not used for shipping or transportation.

> Spain occupies the major part of the Iberian Peninsula and is almost completely surrounded by water. The sea plays a major role in the daily lives of many Spaniards.

MEXICO
Important Cities

México, D.F., is the capital and the business center of the country. With its 20,000,000 inhabitants it is the western hemisphere's most populated city and the cultural center of the nation.

Acapulco is a center of tourism and a popular beach resort on the Pacific Ocean.

Mérida, which lies southeast of the capital, is a site of Mayan architecture and culture.

Saltillo, located in the north central part of the country, enjoys a dry, comfortable climate. It is a university center of the nation.

Veracruz, a fishing center on the Gulf of Mexico, is famous for its distinctive cuisine and lively music.

Mexico is divided into two long vertical sections by a dual mountain chain called the *Sierra Madre*. This has served as a barrier to communication, transportation, and national unification. For those who can't afford to fly, travel through the Sierra Madre is long and difficult.

Important Facts

The Mayans and Aztecs built advanced civilizations long before the arrival of the Spanish.

Over eighty percent of Mexico's population is of Indian origin.

Mexico is the only Spanish-speaking nation in North America.

Mexico's foreign and domestic economy is based heavily on agriculture.

Lack of water is one of Mexico's greatest problems.

The *Río Bravo*—Mexican Spanish for *Río Grande*—forms part of the border between the United States and Mexico and flows into the Gulf of Mexico.

A Write the number of each city next to its name.

_____ Málaga

_____ Barcelona

_____ Granada

_____ Madrid

_____ Sevilla

ESPAÑA

_____ Veracruz

_____ Acapulco

_____ México, D.F.

_____ Mérida

_____ Saltillo

MEXICO

B   Name the cities suggested by the clues below.

1.   Spain's summer playground

   _____

2.   most populated city of North America

   _____

3.   site of the Alhambra

   _____

4.   center of Mayan architecture

   _____

5.   most cosmopolitan city of Spain

   _____

6.   a university center in Mexico

   _____

7.   port city on the Guadalquivir

   _____

8.   fishing port on the Gulf of Mexico

   _____

9.   capital and geographical center of Spain

   _____

10.   a Mexican resort city on the Pacific

   _____

C   **Spain**. After studying the map carefully, find the following items.

1.   the river that flows from west to east   _____

2.   two rivers that flow through Portugal   _____

3.   the mountains dividing France and Spain   _____

4.   the country to the west of Spain   _____

5.   the river on which Sevilla is located   _____

D Match column **B** with column **A**.

A

1. Barcelona _____
2. Tajo _____
3. Pirineos _____
4. Saltillo _____
5. Sevilla _____
6. Río Bravo _____
7. Portugal _____
8. Veracruz _____
9. Ebro _____
10. Granada _____

B

a. Río Grande
b. country to the west of Spain
c. Spain's northern port
d. city on the Guadalquivir
e. longest river in Spain
f. Alhambra
g. Mexican fishing resort
h. university city
i. mountain boundary
j. flows eastward

E Escribe al lado del dibujo el nombre de la ciudad que pertenece. *Write the name of the city suggested by the picture.*

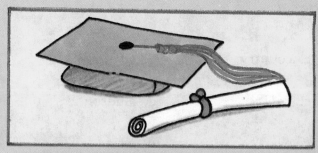

1. _____

2. _____

3. _____

4. _____

5. _____

F Escoge la palabra correcta. *Choose the correct word.*

1. *Sevilla* is a....
   a. river
   b. mountain
   c. country
   d. city
2. Málaga is a port on the....
   a. Mediterranean
   b. Atlantic
   c. Pacific
   d. Hudson
3. The Ebro flows to the....
   a. north
   b. south
   c. east
   d. west
4. The *Pirineos* are....
   a. tribesmen
   b. lakes
   c. cities
   d. mountains
5. The country to the west of Spain is....
   a. France
   b. Portugal
   c. Italy
   d. Russia
6. Mérida is a city in....
   a. Cuba
   b. Chile
   c. Florida
   d. Mexico
7. Toledo is a city on the....
   a. Duero
   b. Ebro
   c. Tajo
   d. Guadiana
8. Saltillo is famous for its....
   a. salt
   b. museums
   c. fishing
   d. universities
9. Veracruz is noted for its....
   a. food and music
   b. politics
   c. desert
   d. churches
10. Granada was a...capital.
    a. Christian
    b. Moorish
    c. Roman
    d. Portuguese

G Write in each blank space the answer that makes each statement geographically correct. Spain is situated at the southwestern tip of Europe, just a short distance from the continent of Africa. 1._____ (*city*), the 2._____, is in the geographical center of the nation. Spain has 3._____ (*number*) major rivers. The 4._____ (*river*) is the only one that flows from 5._____ to 6._____. About two thirds of Spain's coast is bordered by the 7._____ Sea. 8._____ (*city*) in the northeast is the largest 9._____ and Málaga in the 10._____ is another major 11._____. 12._____ is an inland port located on the Guadalquivir. The 13._____ mountains separate 14._____ from 15._____. They are found in the 16._____ (*direction*) part of the country. 17._____, a small country to the 18._____, shares the Iberian Peninsula with Spain. The 19._____ Sea forms the northwestern 20._____ of Spain.

H ## Projects

1. You are a tour guide hired to lead a group of scholars from the United States on a cultural and historical tour of Mexico. Name three cities you would show them and tell what they would see there.

2. Name three places you would like to visit if you were the winner of a three-week vacation in Spain during the winter recess. Tell why you would like to visit each place.

Maze

Marijosé and Miguel are ready to travel. Trace their vacation route to find out where they will be spending the summer. Name their destination in the space provided. List the places they will visit en route.

México, D.F.

Places they'll visit:

Their destination is:

_____

Crucigrama

Vertical

1. site of Mayan ruins
3. Spain's inland port
4. home of the Alhambra
6. university city

Horizontal

1. country and capital with the same name
2. capital of Spain
5. Mexican city famous for music and food
7. Mexican resort on the Pacific
8. Spain's longest river
9. cosmopolitan city in Spain

HOUSE
La casa

Clara: ¿Dónde vives?
Beto: Vivo en una casa en Sevilla.

Where do you live?
I live in a house in Seville.

José: ¿Dónde está el jardín?
Amanda: El jardín está allá.

Where is the garden?
The garden is over there.

Evita: ¿Dónde está el garaje?
Franco: Está detrás del jardín.

Where is the garage?
It's behind the garden.

Luz: ¿Cuántos cuartos hay en tu casa?

How many rooms are there in your house?

Carlos: Hay siete cuartos.

There are seven rooms.

Los cuartos de la casa

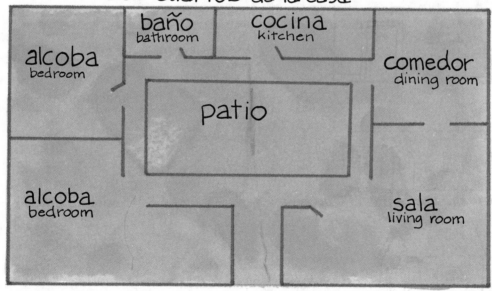

baño
bathroom

cocina
kitchen

alcoba
bedroom

comedor
dining room

patio

alcoba
bedroom

sala
living room

 Cada oveja con su pareja.

Birds of a feather flock together.

1. mansión

2. casa particular

3. edificio de apartamentos

4. apartamento

5. remolque habitable

6. casucha

7. tienda de campaña

A   Escribe el nombre de cada cuarto en español.

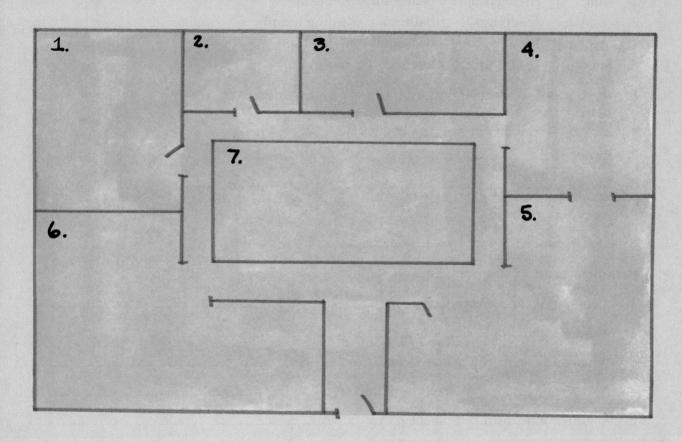

B   Completa las frases.

1. Yo <u>cocino</u> en la _____.
   (cook)

2. Yo <u>duermo</u> en la _____.
   (sleep)

3. Yo <u>como</u> en el _____.
   (eat)

4. Yo <u>me baño</u> en el _____.
   (bathe)

5. Yo <u>juego</u> en el _____.
   (play)

6. Yo <u>descanso</u> en la _____.
   (relax)

C   Escoge el nombre correcto para cada cuarto.

1. cocina   (bedroom   kitchen   bathroom)
2. sala   (living room   bedroom   kitchen)
3. comedor   (bedroom   bathroom   dining room)
4. alcoba   (dining room   bedroom   living room)
5. baño   (bedroom   kitchen   bathroom)

D   In which room would you find a... (En español, por favor.)

1. bathtub? _____

2. dining table? _____

3. sofa? _____

4. stove? _____

5. nightstand? _____

E   Completa cada frase en español.

1. A one-family house is called a _____.

2. A shack or hut is a _____.

3. When one goes camping, one sleeps in a _____.

4. A single unit in an apartment building is an _____.

5. A family on vacation might sleep in a _____.

6. A very wealthy family might live in a _____.

F   Descifra las palabras.

1. INCOAC _____

2. ALAS _____

3. MOODREC _____

4. BACAOL _____

5. OPITA _____

CASA   FAMILIA   AMOR

G Lee el párrafo. Escoge las respuestas correctas.

Mi familia y yo vivimos en una casa bonita. La casa tiene seis cuartos. Hay flores en el patio. Quiero mucho a mi familia.

vivimos = we live	**tiene** = (it) has
hay = there is (are)	**quiero** = I love

1. Mi familia vive en....
   a. un jardín
   c. un cuarto
   b. una casa
   d. un patio

2. La casa es....
   a. bonita
   c. grande
   b. fea
   d. chica

3. La casa tiene...cuartos.
   a. tres
   c. seis
   b. nueve
   d. diez

4. El patio tiene....
   a. cocina
   c. Madrid
   b. baño
   d. flores

H

Vertical

1. where the family eats
2. any room in a house
3. bedroom
5. living room
6. where the shower is
10. "...de campaña"

Horizontal

1. where food is prepared
4. poor family's shack
7. general word for house
8. flower garden, small yard
9. central open courtyard
11. "¿...vives?"
12. rich person's home

LA GUACA
URBANIZACION

Torres del Bosque

Apartamentos de 200 a 450 Mts.²
- El mejor lote con bosque nativo en Bosque Medina.
- Lejos del ruido de la ciudad.

"la casa del ensueño"

Lo mejor bajo el sol...

Su hogar campestre
en el valle de Los Lanceros
Condominio Verdesol, a 3 Kms. de Melgar Vía Carmen de Apicalá

Un tesoro para disfrutar con su familia

- Apartamento de 3 alcobas totalmente alfombrados
- Amplio salón comedor
- Cómoda cocina con zona de ropas
- El sector más recursivo del centro sur de Bogotá
- Completo servicio de transporte
- Excelentes vías de acceso
- Bello diseño arquitectónico con amplio campo visual
- Espaciosas zonas verdes

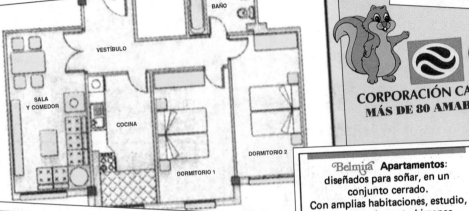

concasa
es su casa
CORPORACIÓN CAFETERA DE AHORRO Y VIVIENDA
MÁS DE 80 AMABLES OFICINAS EN 30 CIUDADES

Belmira **Apartamentos:**
diseñados para soñar, en un conjunto cerrado.
Con amplias habitaciones, estudio, salón comedor con chimenea, Parque Infantil, Cancha de Squash y muchos detalles más, que crean un ambiente acogedor y dan calor de hogar.
Apartamentos desde $ 25'000.000
Financiación a 15 años con Conavi.

Su casa en 90 días!

Construcción tradicional para la casa que usted quiere

PARA USTED

EL PORTAL DEL Nortiño
Carrera 110 No.75D-01

FINANCIACION 80% **CORPAVI**

CASAS MUY:

VISITE CASA MODELO

CERCA
A 1 cuadra de la Autopista Medellín

COMPLETAS
4 alcobas, 2 baños y patio

PRACTICAS
Algunas con local, hasta 93 M.²

ECONOMICAS
Desde **$17'900.000**

Y APARTAMENTOS DE 3 ALCOBAS Y 2 BAÑOS
DESDE $15'400.000

INFORMES Y VENTAS:
CONSTRUCTORA COLMENA
Valoramos su bienestar
Calle 76 No.10-02 Tels.: 2117700 - 2288567

NUEVA IBERIA

Calle 137A No.52-35

Su nuevo apartamento de 2 y 3 alcobas
- Sus zonas verdes
- Su cancha de squash
- La nueva avenida Las Villas

CARACTERISTICAS
- Placa de concreto
- Estructura sismo-resistente
- Cimiento ciclópeo
- Muros en ladrillo hueco
- Pañete rústico
- Cubierta en teja de barro
- Areas sociales en tablón
- Baños enchapados en cerámica
- Habitaciones con sus closets
- Ventanería en madera
- Terraza exterior enmarcada por columnas de madera

Construimos en todo el país

BOGOTA
Diagonal 109 No. 20-60
Tels.: 2143111 - 2142209

CALI
Calle 44 Norte No. 3H-18
Tels.: 649047 - 649048

MEDELLIN
Calle 4 Sur No. 43A-195 Of.249
Tels.: 2685397 - 2667879

BENHABITAT
Constructora
La excelente forma de vivir

La alegría de llegar a casa!
Por sólo $6.800.000

Portales 2
Última Etapa

Calle 168A No. 58-66

10.000 m2 en zonas verdes; zonas de recreación, parques, canchas múltiples, salón comunal en cada manzana.
3 cómodas habitaciones con closets, sala independiente de comedor; magnífica cocina semi-integral, terraza; acabados de primera.

Excelentes vías de acceso,
ANTENA PARABÓLICA.
Casas al mejor precio del mercado.
Sepárela con sólo $100.000
Financiación 70%
A.M.B. 0449 Sep. 28/87

Pablo: ¿Quién es?	Who is it?
Melinda: Es mi <u>hermano</u>.	It's my <u>brother</u>.
Amanda: ¿Quiénes son?	Who are they?
Andrés: Son mis <u>nietos</u>.	They're my <u>grandchildren</u>.
Patricio: ¿Son tus <u>padres</u>?	Are they your <u>parents</u>?
Miguel: Sí, Ana es mi <u>madre</u> y Juan es mi <u>padre</u>.	Yes, Ana is my <u>mother</u>, and Juan is my <u>father</u>.
Luz: Rosita, Paco y Clara son <u>hermanos</u>, ¿no?	Rosita, Paco and Clara are <u>brother and sisters</u>, aren't they?
Lorenzo: Sí, y también son mis <u>primos</u>.	Yes, and they're also my <u>cousins</u>.

Recuerda: Reunión familiar Invitados • abuelo, abuela • mi tía Luisa y su esposo • mi prima Sara • mi primo Beto • mi hermana y sus hijos • Andrés y su esposa • Marta y la nena	Remember: Family Reunion Guests • grandfather, grandmother • Aunt Luisa and her husband • Cousin Sara • Cousin Beto • my sister and her children • Andrés and his wife • Marta and the baby (girl)

Andrés: ¿Dónde están tus <u>parientes</u>?	Where are your <u>relatives</u>?
Cándida: Mis <u>abuelos</u> están adentro y mis <u>tíos</u> están en el jardín.	My <u>grandparents</u> are inside and my <u>aunts</u> and <u>uncles</u> are in the garden.
Guadalupe: ¿Están aquí tus <u>padrinos</u>?	Are your <u>godparents</u> here?
Beto: ¡Cómo no! Mi <u>madrina</u> habla con mis <u>tías</u>. Mi <u>padrino</u> está en el patio.	Of course! My <u>godmother</u> is speaking with my <u>aunts</u>. My <u>godfather</u> is in the patio.
Juanita: ¿Cómo se llaman tus <u>sobrinos</u>?	What are the names of your <u>nephew</u> and <u>niece</u>?
Franco: Mi <u>sobrino</u> es Pedro y mi <u>sobrina</u> es Lupe.	My <u>nephew</u> is Pedro, and my <u>niece</u> is Lupe.
Juanita: ¿Eres tú su único <u>tío</u>?	Are you their only <u>uncle</u>?
Franco: No, Adán también es su tío.	No, Adán is their uncle as well.

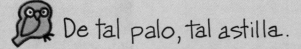 De tal palo, tal astilla. | A chip off the old block.

Paco ———————— Luz

Beto   Evita ——————— Raúl

Pancho   Juanita   Pablo

Exercises

A Indicate Juanita's relationship to each family member listed.

EXAMPLE

Juanita es la

1. _____ hermana _____ de Pancho.
2. _____ de Raúl.
3. _____ de Luz.
4. _____ de Beto.
5. _____ de Pablo.
6. _____ de Evita.
7. _____ de Paco.

B Haz lo mismo para Evita y Paco. *Do the same for Evita and Paco.*

Evita es la

1. _____ de Beto.
2. _____ de Raúl.
3. _____ de Pablo, Pancho y Juanita.
4. _____ de Luz y Paco.

Paco es el

1. _____ de Pablo, Pancho y Juanita.
2. _____ de Luz.
3. _____ de Beto y Evita.

C ¿Quién es...? *Who is...?* (En español, por favor.)

1. el hermano de mi padre

   Es mi _____.

2. la hija de mi tío

   Es mi _____.

3. la madre de mi madre

   Es mi _____.

4. el hijo de mi hermana

   Es mi _____.

5. la madre de mi hermano

   Es mi _____.

D Escoge la respuesta correcta.

1. ¿Dónde están los padres?
   a. on the bench
   b. in the playpen
   c. in the foreground

2. ¿Dónde está la nena?
   a. on the bench
   b. in the playpen
   c. in the foreground

3. ¿Dónde están los abuelos?
   a. on the bench
   b. in the playpen
   c. in the foreground

E ¿Quién soy yo? *Who am I?* (En español, por favor.)

1. I am your nephew's father. In other words, I am your _____.

2. I am your female sibling. In other words, I am your _____.

3. I am your sister's daughter. In other words, I am your _____.

4. I am your mother's father. In other words, I am your _____.

F Escribe en inglés.

1. ¿Quién es? _____

2. ¿Quién soy yo? _____

3. ¿Quién es la profesora? _____

4. ¿Quién prepara la lección? _____

G Completa en español.

1. ¿Quién es la chica?
   Ella es mi _____.

2. ¿Quién es el señor *(man)*?
   Es mi _____.

3. ¿Quién es el chico?
   Es mi _____.

H Lee el párrafo. Escribe el párrafo en inglés.

Mi familia

Mi familia es grande. Mi padre y mi madre tienen treinta y ocho años. Tengo dos hermanos y tres hermanas. Paco, mi hermano mayor, tiene dieciséis años. Mi hermanita Nilda tiene siete años. La familia vive en Santa Rosa.

vivir = to live	**tienen** = have
mayor = older	**tengo** = I have
-ito, -ita = (*diminutive suffix*) little	**tiene** = is (*when used with age*)

8

OCCUPATIONS
Profesiones y empleos

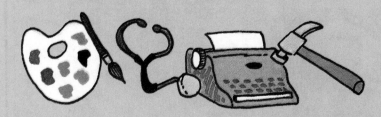

¿Cuál es tu profesión?
   Soy <u>actor</u>.
¿A qué te dedicas?
   Soy <u>actriz</u>.

What is your profession?
I am an <u>actor</u>.
What do you do (for a living)?
I am an <u>actress</u>.

artista   (m.& f.) = artist
cartero   (m.) = mail carrier
comerciante (m.&f.)= businessperson
electricista (m.& f)= electrician
músico   (m.) = musician

Agencia de empleos Acme
Buscamos un(a):

carpintero,-a   mecánico (m.)
cocinero,-a   médico,-a
enfermero,-a   plomero,-a
granjero,-a   profesor,-a

Empleo garantizado.

Tel.   12-59-43

Acme Employment Agency
We are looking for:

carpenter   mechanic
cook   physician
nurse   plumber
farmer   teacher

Work guaranteed.

Tel. 12-59-43

 El ejercicio hace maestro.   Practice makes perfect.

Exercises

A Number in order the professions or trades as the teacher recites them.

el médico _____

el mecánico _____

el cartero _____.

el enfermero _____

el cocinero _____

la comerciante _____

el electricista _____

el granjero _____

B ¿Quién trabaja aquí? *Who works here?*

1. hospital _____

2. stage _____

3. school _____

4. wood shop _____

5. department store _____

6. restaurant _____

7. post office _____

8. garage _____

9. farm _____

10. studio _____

C Descifra las palabras.

1. LOPEROM _____

2. OTCAR _____

3. ITARTAS _____

4. TARCORE _____

5. TARZIC _____

D Write these sentences in English. Look first, then take a good guess.

1. Ana actúa en el teatro.

   _____

2. Mi tío repara autos.

   _____

3. Mi hermano es profesor.

   _____

4. El canta la música.

   _____

5. María estudia electricidad.

   _____

6. Papá es granjero.

   _____

7. Raúl prepara la comida.

   _____

E Guess who... (En español, por favor.)

1. El _____ instructs pupils.

2. La _____ administers to the sick.

3. La _____ paints portraits.

4. El _____ brings the mail.

5. El _____ wires the house for electric power.

6. El _____ repairs motors.

7. La _____ prepares food.

8. El _____ harvests the grain.

9. El _____ plays in a string quartet.

10. El _____ repairs broken pipes.

F   Escribe en español la profesión o empleo que corresponde a cada dibujo.

1. _____

2. _____

3. _____

4. _____

5. _____

PEDRO ALMODOVAR
DIRECTOR DE CINE

Desayuno con churros

Un desayuno muy castizo con un madrileño de pura cepa, nieto de Muñoz Seca, el también escritor y periodista Alfonso Ussía.

NUESTRO LEGADO HISPANO
Haciendo historia cada día

Miriam Alonso
Administradora,
Educadora, Escritora.

Miriam Colón Valle
Actriz, Directora,
Productora.

Margarita Colmenares
Ingeniera.

FOOD
La comida

9

¿Qué tenemos para comer?
Tenemos ensalada.

What do we have to eat?
We have salad.

¿Tienes hambre?
Sí, tengo hambre.

Are you hungry?
Yes, I'm hungry.

¿Tienes sed?
No, no tengo sed.

Are you thirsty?
No, I'm not thirsty.

Bodega de Patricio
Venta de bebidas

Café Caribe (½ kg)	30 pesos
Sangría El Pepe	45 pesos
Leche (un litro)	40 pesos
Chocolate Moctezuma	25 pesos
Agua mineral (2 litros)	40 pesos
Jugos Inca (lata)	35 pesos

Patrick's Grocery
Beverages

"Caribe" coffee ½ kg	30 pesos
"El Pepe" sangria	45 pesos
milk (1 liter)	40 pesos
Montezuma chocolate	25 pesos
Mineral water (2 liters)	40 pesos
Inca fruit juices (can)	35 pesos

El rincón de Juanita
comida típica

Menú del día ——Viernes

Desayuno especial
1. Continental con jugo natural 4 euros
2. Campero
   Dos huevos, pan tostado,
   jamón o salchichas, papas
   Juanita, bebida   9 euros

¡Calidad con sabor!

Joanie's Corner
regional food

Menu of the day—Friday

Breakfast Special
1. "Continental" with fresh juice 4 euro
2. "Farmer"
   Two eggs, toast, ham
   or sausage, Joanie's
   home fried potatoes,
   beverage   9 euro
   Quality with taste!

 A buen hambre,
no hay pan duro.

To a hungry person there is
no hard bread.

naranja
piña
pera
manzana
plátano

breakfast = desayuno
lunch, midday
main meal } = almuerzo
o comida
dinner = cena o comida

Lista de compras   Shopping List

espinacas	spinach
bistec	steak
galletas	cookies
papas	potatoes
tomates	tomatoes
pollo	chicken
queso	cheese
pudín instantáneo	instant pudding
helado	ice cream

la pimienta
pepper

la sal
salt

el florero
vase

la taza
cup

la mantequilla
butter

el vaso
glass

el platillo
saucer

el plato
plate

el azúcar
sugar

la servilleta
napkin

el tenedor
fork

el cuchillo
knife

la cucharita
teaspoon

el mantel
tablecloth

la cuchara
spoon

la mesa
table

Specialties of Spain and Latin America

Spain

Tortilla española—omelet laced with onions and diced potato, served hot as an entrée or eaten cold as a lunch

Paella valenciana—casserole of chicken and seafood served on a bed of saffron rice

Arroz con pollo—chicken and saffron rice served in a sauce seasoned with onion and garlic and cooked with fresh peas

Flan caramelo—custard served with a sauce of slightly burned sugar

Fresas con nata—fresh strawberries served with sweetened heavy whipped cream

Latin America

Ropa vieja (Cuba)—casserole containing ground beef, chicken, sausage, peppers, onions, and garlic in saffron rice

Chile con carne (Mexico)—ground beef, tomatoes, onion, green peppers, and kidney beans seasoned with chile powder

Churros—long doughnuts served with chocolate

Chocolate (Mexico)—thick hot chocolate often eaten with a spoon or used for dunking churros

Tacos (Mexico)—folded tortillas (corn flour pancakes) often filled with chile-flavored meat, refried beans, lettuce, tomatoes, cheese, and so on

"¡Buen provecho!"—a wish on the part of a friend or host that all the guests may enjoy the meal and eat heartily

Exercises

A Escribe el nombre de cada objeto en español.

1. _____

2. _____

3. _____

4. _____

5. _____

6. _____

B Completa cada frase en inglés.

1. A custard dessert quite popular in Spain is _____.

2. "Ropa vieja" is a casserole of assorted meats and vegetables originating in

   _____.

3. The two basic ingredients found in "arroz con pollo" are _____

   and _____.

4. A Mexican dish of ground beef, tomatoes, onions, green peppers, and kidney beans

   seasoned with chile powder is called _____.

5. "Ropa vieja," "tacos," and "chile con carne" are three popular foods in

   _____.

C Write three food items for each of the following categories.

<table>
<tr><td align="center">meat</td><td align="center">vegetables</td></tr>
<tr><td>1. _____</td><td>1. _____</td></tr>
<tr><td>2. _____</td><td>2. _____</td></tr>
<tr><td>3. _____</td><td>3. _____</td></tr>
<tr><td align="center">dairy products</td><td align="center">beverages</td></tr>
<tr><td>1. _____</td><td>1. _____</td></tr>
<tr><td>2. _____</td><td>2. _____</td></tr>
<tr><td>3. _____</td><td>3. _____</td></tr>
<tr><td align="center">fruits</td><td align="center">desserts</td></tr>
<tr><td>1. _____</td><td>1. _____</td></tr>
<tr><td>2. _____</td><td>2. _____</td></tr>
<tr><td>3. _____</td><td>3. _____</td></tr>
</table>

D   **Projects**

Answer either 1 or 2 *and* 3 or 4.

1. You are opening a restaurant in Latin America. From your food list, prepare a menu for lunch and dinner. At least five dishes for each meal should be offered. Specialty dishes may be used.
2. Prepare a poster from magazine pictures. Show a balanced breakfast and a balanced dinner. Label each food item with its Spanish name.
3. Prepare fifteen different flashcards each with a picture of a food item on one side and its Spanish name on the other.
4. In Spanish, list fifteen words that name foods. Then scramble each word. These can be used in classroom games. Examples: LECHE = EHLCE / CAFE = AFCE

Crucigrama

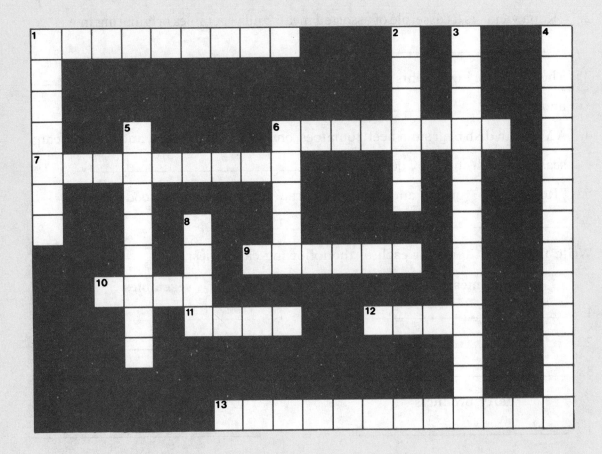

E

Vertical

1. enjoyed with chocolate
2. where tacos originated
3. Mexican beef-vegetable dish
4. Spanish chicken casserole
5. sauce served over flan
6. meat- and vegetable-filled corn cakes
8. popular Spanish dessert

Horizontal

1. beverage from Mexico
6. Spanish word for omelet
7. Cuban casserole
9. where paella and flan are popular
10. what is set for meals
11. served over "fresas"
12. country of origin, "ropa vieja"
13. dinnertime wish

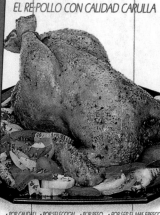

Three Great Artists

El Greco, Doménikos Theotokópoulos (1541–1614), was born on the isle of Crete. He studied art in Venice, Italy, before going to Spain in 1577. He settled in Toledo under the sponsorship of the governor, for whom he painted many religious works. The artistic style used by El Greco has been called realistic mysticism, an art style that began in Spain with him. It is characterized by the elongated and delicate traits of the human body. The good people look as if they could almost float to heaven. A simple formula for this style is: *light and delicate: good = darkness and bulk: evil.* The *Burial of the Count of Orgaz* is one of El Greco's masterpieces.

Diego Velázquez (1599–1660) is the father of Spanish realism. His successful career began at the age of twenty when he painted *The Water Carrier of Seville.* Several years later he was appointed royal court artist, a position he held until his death. Velázquez is famous for the way he painted the people and objects around him. He made them look real. He treated noblemen, tradesmen, and peasants with dignity and respect. By using color and light skillfully, he gave life and feeling to all his paintings. Velázquez is the greatest Spanish artist of the classical era.

Francisco de Goya was born near Zaragoza. He went to Madrid at twenty-seven and soon became famous as a master of two styles of art, the rococo and the neobaroque.

Goya painted the social customs of Spanish peasant life. He also painted the royal court and the innocent victims of the Napoleonic forces of France. Later in life, Goya became depressed by the world around him and began to paint people and things in a distorted and ugly way. Discouraged by the cruelty around him, he went to France, where he died in 1828. *The Parasol* is one of his best paintings.

A caballo regalado no se le mira el diente.

Never look a gift horse in the mouth.

The Burial of the Count of Orgaz
(oil on canvas, 1586)
by El Greco
Catedral de Santo Tomás, Toledo, Spain

The Water Carrier of Seville
(oil on canvas, 1619–20)
by Diego Velázquez
Victoria and Albert Museum, London

Don Manuel Osorio de Zúñiga
(oil on canvas, 1788)
by Francisco de Goya
The Metropolitan Museum of Art, New York

The Parasol
(oil on canvas, 1777)
by Francisco de Goya
Museo del Prado, Madrid

Exercises

A Name the picture that shows:

1. a man selling water. _____

2. a nobleman being buried in the church. _____

3. a young prince at play. _____

B Name the Spanish artist whose works reveal:

1. light and darkness as symbols. _____

2. realistic portrayal of the human body. _____

3. pastoral scenes. _____

4. a spiritualized human form. _____

5. lighting and color reflecting reality. _____

6. people and things painted in a distorted manner. _____

C Asocia la frase en inglés con el nombre en español.

A	B
1. Toledo _____	a. mystical painting
2. Goya _____	b. father of Spanish realism
3. Velázquez _____	c. Doménikos Theotokópoulos
4. El Greco _____	d. home of El Greco
5. *The Burial of the Count of Orgaz* _____	e. painter of rural life

D Complete the analogies.

1. Madrid: Velázquez = Toledo: _____

2. country life: _____ = court life: Velázquez

3. Velázquez: realism = El Greco: _____

4. governor: El Greco = _____: Velázquez

E ¿Qué nombre corresponde al dibujo?

El Greco

Velázquez

Goya

F Which artist would most likely be...

1. attending an elaborate church ceremony? _____

2. using a live horse for exact proportion? _____

3. painting peasants at work and play? _____

G In your opinion...

1. whose paintings could decorate a Gothic cathedral?

_____

2. whose paintings show things as they really are?

_____

3. whose paintings show how poor country people live?

_____

H Which of the paintings in this unit do you like best? _____

Who created this masterpiece? _____

State in your own words what the picture is about and why you like it.

_____

_____

_____

_____

_____

I Escribe las palabras que faltan.

1. Diego _____ worked in the Royal Palace in

_____ .

2. El Greco was sponsored by the _____ of

_____ .

3. Francisco _____ was born in Zaragoza and worked in

_____ .

ARTE DEL RENACIMIENTO

Museo del Prado, España

ARTE GÓTICO EN ESPAÑA

La galería de la Calle Cristo

El Amolador de Guillermo Rodríguez García

Tel. 977-4266

Calle Cristo #156, Viejo San Juan
(segundo nivel **Stylo**)

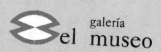

**OBRAS DE ARTE
GRANDES MAESTROS**

el museo
galería

Botero, Obregón, Grau, Wiedemann, Caballero, Roda y otros maestros nacionales e internacionales, cómprelos a quien garantice su precio y legitime su autenticidad. GALERIA EL MUSEO, abierto de lunes a viernes, 10:00 a.m. a 1:00 p.m. y 3:00 p.m. a 7:00 p.m.; sábado 11:00 a.m. a 5:00 p.m., jornada continua. Calle 84 No. 13 - 17, Bogotá. Teléfonos:
2566527 - 2566947.

Barrio de los Artistas

Joan Miró

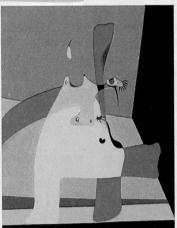

Recuerdo
Souvenir

MUSEO

Picasso

BARCELONA

EL ARTE ROMÁNICO EN ESPAÑA

PARTS OF THE BODY
Las partes del cuerpo

la cabeza

el cuello

el hombro

el codo [

el pecho

el brazo

el estómago

la mano

la pierna

la rodilla

el pie

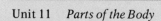
Una mano lava la otra.

One hand washes the other.

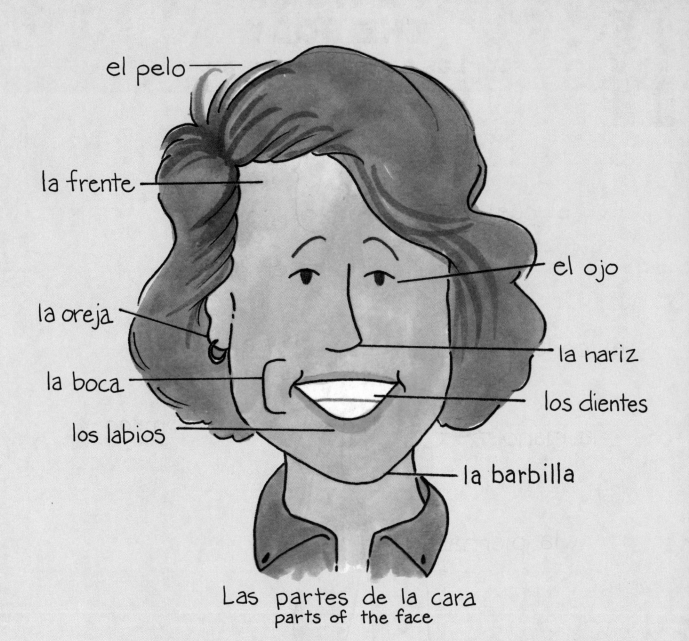

el pelo

la frente

la oreja

la boca

los labios

el ojo

la nariz

los dientes

la barbilla

Las partes de la cara
parts of the face

el dedo = the finger	
el dedo (del pie) = the toe	
el diente = the tooth	
el labio = the lip	

Exercises

A   Label the parts of the body. (En español, por favor.)

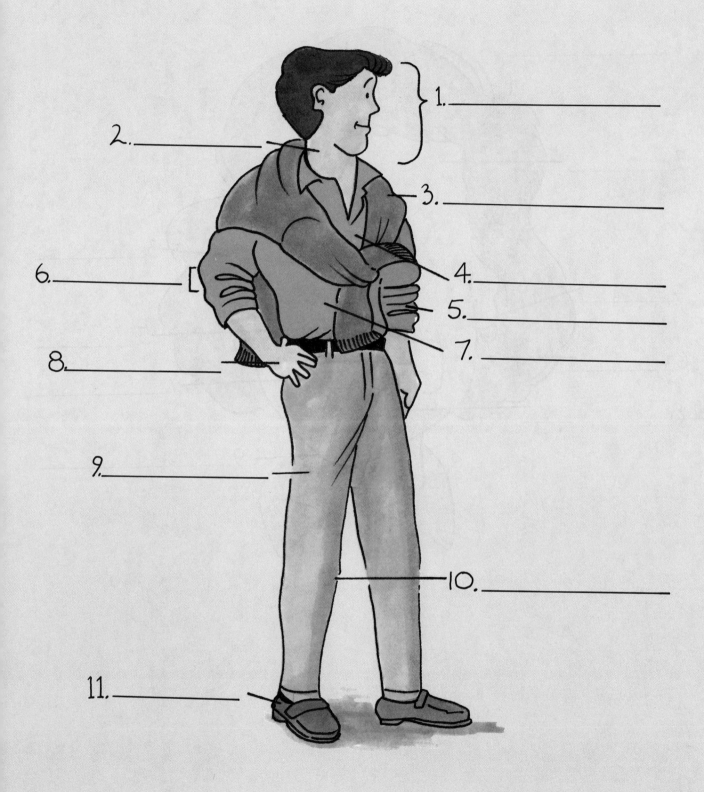

1._____

2._____

3._____

4._____

5._____

6._____

7._____

8._____

9._____

10._____

11._____

B   Label the parts of the face. (En español, por favor.)

1. _____

2. _____

3. _____

4. _____

5. _____

6. _____

7. _____

8. _____

9. _____

C Complete the analogies.

1. la rodilla: la pierna = _____ : el brazo

2. _____ : el pie = el brazo: la pierna

3. los dedos: _____ = los dedos del pie: el pie

4. los labios: la boca = el pelo: _____

D Completa cada frase en español.

1. We see with our _____ .

2. The tongue is in the _____ .

3. The _____ helps us listen.

4. The pen is held in the _____ .

5. The _____ are needed to chew food.

6. The toes are found on the _____ .

7. We use the _____ to smell a rose.

8. We play a guitar with our _____ .

9. The "funny bone" is located on the _____ .

10. Digestion takes place chiefly in the _____ .

E Guess the meaning of the underlined verbs.

1. Yo hablo con la boca. _____

2. Yo toco con el dedo. _____

3. Yo veo con el ojo. _____

4. Yo oigo con la oreja. _____

5. Yo huelo con la nariz. _____

F   Name the part of the body associated with each illustration. (En español, por favor.)

1. _____

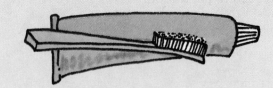

2. _____

3. _____

¡Qué idea!

4. _____

5. _____

6. _____

7. _____

8. _____

9. _____

10. _____

G Asocia la palabra en inglés con la palabra en español. (*Match the activity in column* **B** *with the Spanish word in column* **A**.)

A	B
1. mano _____	a. kneeling
2. ojos _____	b. smelling
3. orejas _____	c. thinking
4. boca _____	d. speaking
5. cabeza _____	e. walking
6. dedos _____	f. writing
7. brazo _____	g. listening
8. rodillas _____	h. touching
9. nariz _____	i. seeing
10. pies _____	j. carrying

H Lee el párrafo. Escoge las respuestas correctas.

Mi cuerpo es una máquina fantástica. Tengo dos orejas, dos ojos, dos labios, dos brazos, dos manos, dos piernas y dos pies. Tengo una cabeza, una nariz y una lengua. Mi cuerpo tiene veinte dedos y treinta y dos dientes. Mi cabeza controla mi cuerpo. Mi cuerpo es maravilloso, ¿no?

máquina = machine

1. Mi cuerpo es....
   a. un animal　　　　　　b. una máquina
   c. una institución　　　 d. un desastre

2. Tengo dos....
   a. brazos　　　　　　　 b. cabezas
   c. dientes　　　　　　　 d. lenguas

3. Mi cuerpo tiene más (*more*) de diez....
   a. narices　　　　　　　 b. pies
   c. ojos　　　　　　　　　d. dientes

4. Mi cabeza controla mi....
   a. nariz　　　　　　　　 b. pies
   c. cuerpo　　　　　　　　d. lengua

5. Mi cuerpo es....
   a. enorme　　　　　　　 b. fantástico
   c. pobre　　　　　　　　 d. elegante

CLOTHING
La ropa

¿Qué llevas?
Llevo mi ropa nueva.

What are you wearing?
I am wearing my new clothes.

Lini
Vacaciones de invierno
Chile — julio

Iberia Santiago

2 vestidos de lana
3 sombreros
3 pares de pijamas
2 cinturones   3 camisas
12 pañuelos   2 blusas
 2 suéteres de lana
   calcetines   abrigo
   guantes
   pantalones
   zapatos

Lini
Winter Vacation
Chile — July

Iberia Santiago

2 woolen dresses
3 hats
3 pairs of pajamas
2 belts   3 shirts
12 handkerchiefs   2 blouses
2 woolen sweaters
   socks   overcoat
   gloves
   pants
   shoes

Modas de Susana
ropa exterior e interior

blusa

vestido

corbata

chaqueta

bata

traje

falda

zapatillas

camisa

Ayer ranchero, hoy caballero.

Clothes make the man.

Exercises

A Asocia la palabra en inglés con la palabra en español.

A	**B**
1. abrigo _____	a. skirt
2. pañuelo _____	b. suit
3. chaqueta _____	c. sweater
4. sombrero _____	d. bathrobe
5. falda _____	e. dress
6. traje _____	f. handkerchief
7. zapatos _____	g. jacket
8. vestido _____	h. hat
9. bata _____	i. overcoat
10. suéter _____	j. shoes

B What do you wear...(En español, por favor.)

1. to a symphony? _____

2. to bed? _____

3. to school? _____

4. in cold weather? _____

5. in cool weather? _____

C Complete the analogies.

1. guantes: manos = _____: pies

2. _____: falda = camisa: pantalones

3. corbata: camisa = _____: pantalones

D ¿Qué llevas?

1. Llevo un _____.

2. Llevo un _____.

3. Llevo una _____.

4. Llevo una _____

   y una _____.

5. Llevo una _____

   y una _____.

E Escribe las palabras en inglés.

1. llevar _____

2. lleva _____

3. llevo _____

4. llevas _____

F Completa en inglés.

1. An "abrigo" goes (under / over) _____ a suit coat.

2. A "blusa" is worn with a _____.

3. A "cinturón" is worn on one's _____.

4. The "zapatos" are worn on the _____.

5. A "corbata" is worn with a _____.

G List the required number of items for each category. (En español, por favor.)

outerwear (5)

_____

_____

_____

_____

_____

accessories (3)

_____

_____

_____

footwear (3)

_____

_____

_____

sleepwear (1)

_____

H Lee el párrafo. Escoge las respuestas correctas.

Esta noche yo asisto al concierto de música clásica con mis padres. Llevo un traje nuevo, una camisa y una corbata. Como hace frío, llevo un abrigo sobre mi ropa nueva. Llevo también los guantes nuevos.

> **tiempo** = weather
> **Hace frío.** = It's cold.

1. ¿A qué función asisto yo esta noche?
   a. una función musical
   b. un circo
   c. una clase de inglés

2. ¿Qué llevo?
   a. una blusa
   b. una sonrisa
   c. un traje

3. ¿Qué tiempo hace?
   a. frío
   b. calor
   c. buen tiempo

4. ¿Qué llevo sobre mi ropa?
   a. ropa interior
   b. un abrigo
   c. un vestido

Crucigrama

Vertical

2. worn over a coat
3. sleepwear
4. worn when a jacket is too warm
5. often worn with a skirt
9. pants, jacket, and vest of the same color
11. hat
12. often worn with a blouse
14. includes all articles of clothing
15. worn over nightwear

Horizontal

1. feet protectors
6. secures pants
7. hand warmers
8. woman's outer garment
10. trousers
13. short hosiery
16. indoor footwear
17. neckwear
18. handkerchief

Calcetines

Zapatos de piel para niños,
con piso de goma.
Tallas 30 a 39,
~~3.390~~
2.595

Chaquetas tallas 2-6 $ 13.000
MULTIOFERTA $ 9.990

Chaqueta sport, camisa en índigo,
jean clásico cinco bolsillos y cinturón.

Chaqueta
con cremallera,
tallas 6 a 18,
~~2.975~~
1.995

Pantalón
a cuadros,
tallas 6 a 18,
~~2.975~~
1.995

Pantalones

Jean T. 28 a 38
Precio Normal: $19.500
MULTIOFERTA $11.750

Unicentro Bogotá *Unicentro Cali* *Galerías Bogotá*

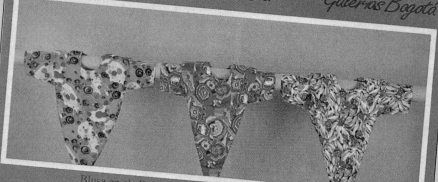

Blusa en chalis estampada. Cuello redondo, manga corta.
Precio Normal: $14.990
MULTIOFERTA $9.990

Corbatas
Precio Normal: $9.990
MULTIOFERTA $4.990

86

TIME
AND COLORS
La hora y los colores

¿Qué hora es?   What time is it?

Es la una y media.

Son las diez
menos cuarto.

Son las tres.

Es mediodía.

¿A qué hora?   At what time...?

A las siete y cuarto.

A medianoche.

A las dos y cinco.

A las doce menos
cinco.

"Es" is used with "la una," "mediodía," and "medianoche."
Transportation in Europe operates on official time, which is on a twenty-four hour basis. Official time is often used by schools, radio and television stations, theaters and movie theaters.

 Más vale tarde que nunca.   Better late than never.

¿De qué color es...?   What color is...?
    Es...   It is...
¿De qué color son...? What color are...?
    Son...   They are...

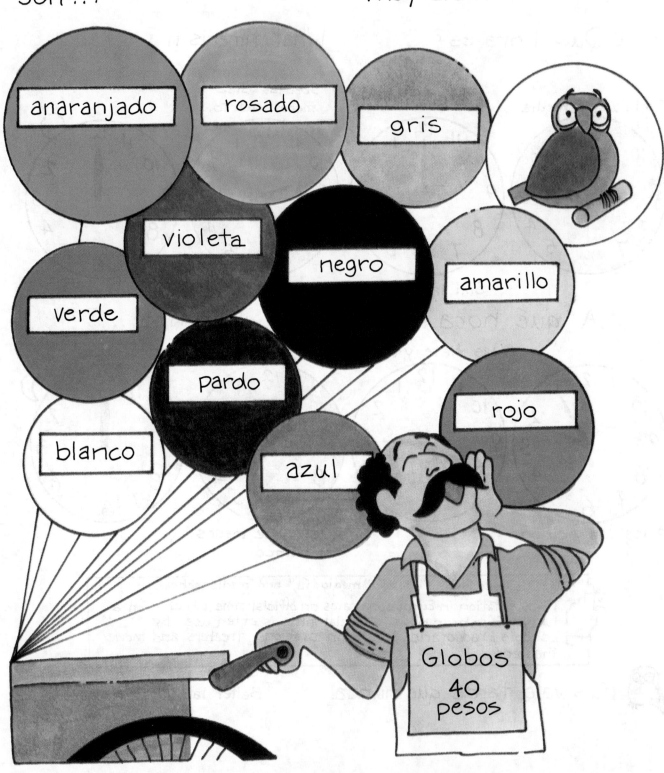

A Listen as your teacher indicates a time. Find the clock that shows that time, and label it number 1. Then your teacher will express another time. Mark the clock expressing that time number 2. Continue until all eight clocks are numbered.

B Completa cada frase en español.

1. The colors of the American flag are _____, _____, and _____.

2. In spring the grass is very _____.

3. When the weather is pleasant, the sky is azure or _____.

4. A shade produced by mixing "negro" and "blanco" is _____.

5. Lemons and dandelions are _____.

6. Flour is _____.

7. Tar is _____.

8. A carrot is _____.

9. Chocolate icing is _____.

10. A color attained by blending "rojo" and "blanco" is _____.

Escribe en español.

1. at one o'clock _____

2. It's half past four. _____

3. at 5:25 _____

4. It's 7:45. _____

5. at a quarter after nine _____

Asocia el español con el inglés.

1. milk or snow _____   a. verde

2. a strawberry _____   b. azul

3. tar or a tire _____   c. blanco

4. a forget-me-not or a robin's egg _____   d. rojo

5. spinach _____   e. negro

Lee el párrafo. Escoge las respuestas correctas.

Paco García va al cine con su amiga Marisela. La película comienza a las ocho. Paco va a llevar su nuevo traje azul, una camisa blanca y una corbata roja. Marisela va a llevar su blusa amarilla con calcetines amarillos y una nueva falda verde. Los dos llevan zapatos negros. Son las seis y media de la tarde y Paco va a la casa de Marisela.

va = he / she goes	**va a llevar** = is going to wear
van = they go	**película** = film

1. La amiga de Paco es...
   a. su madre.   b. Raúl.
   c. su hermana.   d. Marisela.

2. Paco y Marisela van al...
   a. museo.   b. teatro.
   c. parque.   d. cine.

3. La corbata de Paco es...
   a. verde.   b. roja.
   c. azul.   d. blanca.

4. Los calcetines de Marisela son...
   a. amarillos.   b. rojos.
   c. negros.   d. grises.

5. Paco va a la casa de Marisela...
   a. a las 7:15.   b. a las 6:45.
   c. a las 6:30.   d. a las 8:00.

Son las 9:00.

Color the clock according to the directions.

1. Color the "pies"   ROJO.
2. Color the "cara"   PARDO.
3. Color the "dientes"   AZUL.
4. Color the "ojos"   VERDE.
5. Color the "pelo"   BLANCO.
6. Color the "nariz"   ROJO.
7. Color the "siete"   GRIS.
8. Color the "dos"   ANARANJADO.
9. Color the "ceros"   VIOLETA.
10. Color the "nueve"   ROSADO.
11. Color the "uno"   NEGRO.
12. Color the "tres."   AMARILLO.

LLENA TU CASA CON LOS COLORES DE LA NAVIDAD

HOROSCOPO: ¿DE QUÉ COLOR SERÁN SUS DÍAS?

	LUNES	MARTES	MIERCOLES	JUEVES	VIERNES	SABADO	DOMINGO
ROMANCE							
AMIGOS							
FAMILIA							
$DINERO$							
PROFESION							
SALUD							
ENERGIA FISICA							

¿QUÉ QUIERE DECIR EL COLOR?

★ SUPERIOR
☆ EXCELENTE
★ MUY BIEN
★ REGULAR
☆ NO MUY BIEN
★ FATAL, HORRIBLE

CARACOL

9.30 Club 10

6.00 Punky Brewster
6.30 Mi pequeño pony
7.00 Teletubbies
Infantil
8.00 Looney Toons
Infantil Dibujos animados
8.30 La Hora Warner
Las mejores caricaturas
9.30 Club 10
Sigue las aventuras de Zeta, Pap, Rap, Abril y Florecita, acompañados por Dinodoro y Cheveronni
12.30 Caracol Noticias
Dirige: Yamid Amat
1.00 Los Simpson
Dibujos animados
2.00 Animaniacs
Infantil
3.00 Pinky y Cerebro
Infantil
4.00 Pokémon
Seriado Dibujos animados
5.00 Mortal Kombat
Seriado de acción
6.00 Sábados felices
Humorístico
7.00 Caracol Noticias
Noticiero dirigido por Yamid Amat
7.30 Sábados felices
Comedia Dirige Jota Mario Valencia
9.00 También caerás
Humorístico con Hernán Orjuela
10.30 Pregunta Yamid
11.00 Cara a Cara
11.30 La dama del pantano
Con Juanita Acosta y Juan Carlos Vargas

RCN

7.30 Esta boca es mía

6.00 Oki Doki
Juvenil
7.00 Clásicos de la diversión
8.00 Barney
Infantil
8.30 Iron Man
Extranjero
9.00 Oliver Twist
Serie
9.30 Televantas
Infantil Vea en este espacio Planeta Tecno, los X-men, el Hombre Araña, Garfield y otros.
Presenta: Mauricio Quintero
12.30 Noticias RCN
Informativo
1.00 Hechizada
1.30 Mi bella genio
2.00 Sabor a limón
3.00 O todos en la cama
4.00 Nuestro Cine
Película Largometraje extranjero. Título sin confirmar
6.00 Hércules
Serie de aventuras
7.00 Noticias RCN
Informativo nacional
7.30 Esta boca es mía
Los mejores artistas en vivo Claudia Elena Vásquez
9.30 Archivos X
Seriado Con Gillian Anderson
10.30 Esta noche sí
Con Pilar Castaño
11.30 Cybill
Seriado extranjero

MUSIC
La música

Three Great Musicians

Antonio Soler (1729–83), a contemporary of Bach and Vivaldi's, is Spain's foremost baroque musician. His music displays the movement, vigor, and counterpoint that are the characteristics of the baroque style.

Like Vivaldi, he was both a priest and a composer. His organ compositions were created almost exclusively for church functions.

Like Bach, he was an expert on both the organ and the harpsichord. Several of his superb sonatas for the harpsichord are still performed by many modern symphony orchestras. Soler, like Bach, was an expert on organ construction. His suggestions were employed in constructing organs for several European cathedrals. His most noted works are entitled *Sonatas for the Harpsichord.*

Juan Crisóstomo Arriaga (1806–26) is the father of the classical movement in Spain and its most celebrated composer. He is called the "Spanish Mozart" because his short life, his musical style, and his great achievements parallel the life of Mozart. Arriaga wrote his first opera at the age of twelve without the help of formal training in harmony. At that same age he began violin studies and at sixteen was recognized as a virtuoso. In 1823 he studied music in Paris and was recognized as a genius.

Arriaga wrote an opera, a symphony, chamber music and church music. His most famous works include *Symphony in D, Quartets for Strings*, and Spain's most famous piece of church music, *Et vitam venturi.*

Manuel de Falla (1876–1946) was born in Cádiz. He studied music at the National Conservatory of Madrid. In 1905 his opera *La vida breve* earned him his nation's highest honor. This musical genius incorporated popular music into almost all the classical forms. His operas, ballets, and concertos are precise and lively. The music of de Falla has wide appeal because of its use of the popular music of his time. *La vida breve, El sombrero de tres picos*, and *Fantasía bética* are three of his compositions. Manuel de Falla was a contemporary of Maurice Ravel, Aaron Copland, and Samuel Barber's.

 El que canta, sus males espanta.   Singing frightens troubles away.

Exercises

A Give the full name and the dates of the composer who...

1. used popular music in his compositions. _____

2. wrote music for the harpsichord and built organs. _____

3. was a boy genius and expert violinist. _____

B Asocia columna **B** con columna **A**.

A

1. Juan Arriaga _____
2. *Et vitam venturi* _____
3. Antonio Soler _____
4. *El sombrero de tres picos* _____
5. Manuel de Falla _____

B

a. baroque harpsichordist
b. used popular themes in classical forms
c. "Spanish Mozart"
d. Spanish church music
e. a famous ballet

C Guess who was...

1. a violin virtuoso? _____

2. a teacher of the organ? _____

3. an expert on organ construction? _____

4. a composer of ballet music? _____

5. the writer of a famous church song? _____

D Complete the analogies.

1. Soler: organ = _____: violin

2. *Et vitam venturi*: Arriaga = *El sombrero de tres picos*: _____

3. _____: baroque music = De Falla: modern music

4. Soler: Bach = Arriaga: _____

5. _____: Soler = Manuel: De Falla

E Add the names of Soler, Arriaga, and De Falla to the lists of their contemporaries.

1. Mozart, Haydn, Cherubini _____

2. Bach, Vivaldi, Handel _____

3. Ravel, Copland, Barber _____

F ¿Qué nombre corresponde a cada dibujo?

Arriaga

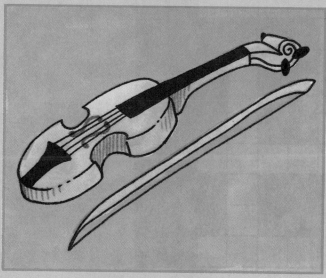

Soler

De Falla

G Descifra las palabras.

1. NOOTINA _____

2. AJNU _____

3. ULEMNA _____

4. LORES _____

5. AFLALED _____

Crucigrama

H

Vertical	Horizontal
1. contemporary of Bach and Vivaldi's	2. place where Soler's music was performed
2. birthplace of modern composer	3. nationally acclaimed opera
4. *Et* _____ *venturi*, church music by Arriaga	7. first name of Spanish baroque musician
5. *El sombrero de tres picos*	8. first name of violin virtuoso
6. the "Spanish Mozart"	

El mes pasado, estuvimos con **Enrique Iglesias** todo un día. Si quieres saber más sobre su último trabajo, no leas esta entrevista. Pero si eres fanática... ¡no te la pierdas!

El Planeta Rock

SHAKIRA

¿Dónde están los ladrones?

Ciudad de México, México

¿Qué tiempo hace?   How's the weather?

Hace buen tiempo.   Más o menos.   Hace mal tiempo.

Hace sol.	It's sunny.	Hace fresco.	It's cool.	Hace frío.	It's cold.
Hace calor.	It's warm.	Hace viento.	It's windy.	Relampaguea.	There's lightning.
		Está húmedo.	It's humid.	Nieva.	It's snowing.
		Está nublado.	It's cloudy.	Truena.	It's thundering.
				Llueve.	It's raining.

¿En qué estación estamos?   What's the season?
Estamos en...   It's ....

Las cuatro estaciones

la primavera

el otoño

el invierno

el verano

 When "en" is used before a season, omit "el" or "la."

 A mal tiempo, buena cara.   A smile brightens a cloudy day.

A ¿Qué frase corresponde a cada dibujo?

1. _____   a. Hace sol.

2. _____   b. Relampaguea.

3. _____   c. Llueve.

4. _____   d. Hace viento.

5. _____   e. Hace frío.

B ¿Qué tiempo hace? Contesta la pregunta en español.

1. _____

2. _____

3. _____

4. _____

5. _____

C ¿Qué estación corresponde a cada dibujo?

1. _____   a. verano

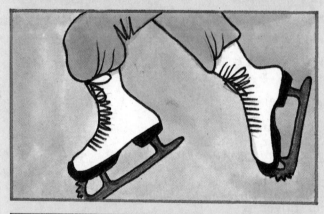

2. _____   b. invierno

3. _____   c. primavera

4. _____   d. otoño

D In **column 1**, write the English meaning of each Spanish word. When you have finished the entire column, cover the column of words at the left, and in **column 2**, change the English words into Spanish.

	column 1 (English)	column 2 (Spanish)
1. sol		
2. relámpago		
3. primavera		
4. verano		
5. tiempo		
6. otoño		
7. estación		
8. fresco		
9. calor		
10. Llueve.		
11. invierno		
12. mal		
13. trueno		
14. frío		

E Asocia la columna **A** con la columna **B**.

A	B
1. lluvia _____	a. hacer sol
2. nieve _____	b. tronar
3. trueno _____	c. relampaguear
4. relámpago _____	d. nevar
5. sol _____	e. llover

F ¿Qué tiempo hace? *Using the cue at the left, write a statement about the weather.* (En español, por favor.)

1. (mittens and parka) _____.

2. (umbrella) _____.

3. (sunglasses) _____.

4. (snowflakes) _____.

5. (lightning bolts) _____.

6. (air conditioner) _____.

7. (cardigan sweater) _____.

8. (sailboat) _____.

9. (outdoor tennis court) _____.

10. (rain, wind, and hail) _____.

G Lee el párrafo. Escoge las respuestas correctas.

Las cuatro estaciones

En primavera hace fresco y llueve mucho. Todo está verde. En verano hace mucho calor. Hace sol casi todos los días. En otoño hace fresco y hace mucho viento. En invierno hace frío y nieva mucho. Las cuatro estaciones son interesantes.

todo = everything

1. El invierno es...
   a. caluroso.   b. verde.
   c. frío.   d. rojo.

2. En primavera todo está...
   a. verde.   b. caluroso.
   c. interesante.   d. frío.

3. Hace fresco en...
   a. verano.   b. invierno.
   c. primavera y otoño.   d. Madrid.

4. Hay...estaciones.
   a. seis   b. tres
   c. cuatro   d. catorce

Crucigrama

H

Vertical

1. cooler than cool
2. "...buen tiempo."
3. light and heat source
4. what skiers like to say
7. when the storm speaks
8. season of roses
9. Summer is a "..." of the year.
11. when it's cold and snowy
12. "Hace mal...."

Horizontal

1. slightly "frío"
4. "Está...."
5. harvest season (*temperate zone*)
6. when showers fall
10. when the sky sparkles and blazes
13. "A mal tiempo, buena...."
14. "En marzo hace...."
15. nature's rebirth
16. damp and clammy
17. opposite of "frío"

El pronóstico de 5 días para Quito

Hoy	Lunes	Martes	Miércoles	Jueves

Parcialmente soleado, con posible aguacero.	Parcialmente soleado, con algunos posibles aguaceros.	Períodos nublados y soleados.	Períodos nublados y soleados.	Parcialmente soleado, con algunos posibles aguaceros.
22 11	21 11	21 11	22 12	21 11

El tiempo para Ecuador

Ibarra 28/16
Quito 22/11
Lago Agrio 32/23
Manta 31/24
Portoviejo 32/23
Ambato 25/14
Riobamba 22/13
Guayaquil 32/24
Cuenca 28/18
Machala 33/25

Este es el tiempo para hoy. Las temperaturas muestran el máximo del día y el mínimo de la noche.

Ciudades de Ecuador

Ciudad	Hoy Máx/Mín/T	Mañana Máx/Mín/T	Pas. Mañana Máx/Mín/T
Ambato	25/14/ch	23/12/ch	25/14/pn
Cuenca	28/18/ll	28/16/ll	28/18/pn
Guayaquil	32/24/pn	32/24/pn	32/24/ll
Portoviejo	32/23/pn	32/23/pn	32/23/ll

Mareas

OTOÑO JUNTO AL MAR
Mar de Ajó, San Bernardo y General Lavalle

Sol y fases de la Luna

	Amanecer	Atardecer	cuarto creciente	luna llena	cuarto menguante	luna nueva
Hoy:	6:15 a.m.	6:22 p.m.	Abr 3	Abr 11	Abr 19	Abr 26
Mañana:	6:15 a.m.	6:22 p.m.				

Ciudades del Mundo

Ciudad	Hoy Máx/Mín/T	Mañana Máx/Mín/T	Pas. Mañana Máx/Mín/T	Ciudad	Hoy Máx/Mín/T	Mañana Máx/Mín/T	Pas. Mañana Máx/Mín/T
Bogotá	17/14/t	17/11/t	22/11/s	Ciudad de México	30/13/s	26/13/pn	28/13/s
Buenos Aires	22/12/s	21/10/pn	21/12/pn	Miami	28/22/pn	29/23/pn	29/23/pn
Cali	27/24/ll	26/22/t	31/22/pn	Montevideo	21/13/s	19/11/pn	18/12/pn
Caracas	30/20/pn	29/21/pn	31/21/pn	Nueva York	26/12/pn	23/9/pn	22/11/pn
La Paz	26/10/s	24/11/s	25/11/pn	Panamá	32/24/ch	32/24/c	34/24/pn
Lima	28/21/t	27/22/c	29/22/pn	París	17/13/c	19/13/c	19/8/pn
Londres	14/11/c	17/14/t	19/11/ch	Río de Janeiro	26/20/s	29/24/pn	29/23/pn
Los Angeles	16/3/ch	15/4/pn	19/7/pn	Santiago	24/4/s	24/9/s	27/11/pn
Madrid	20/14/ch	19/9/t	18/6/pn	Santo Domingo	28/22/t	28/21/t	30/21/pn

Tiempo(T): **s**-soleado, **pn**-parcialmente nublado, **c**-nublado, **ch**-chubascos, **t**-tormentas, **ll**-lluvia, **ni**-nieve intermitente, **nv**-nieve, **h**-hielo.

Todos los mapas, pronósticos e información son proporcionados por AccuWeather, Inc.   http://www.accuweather.com

¿Qué día es hoy?
Hoy es...

What day is today?
Today is....

Monday lunes	martes	miércoles	jueves	viernes	sábado	domingo
	1	2	3	4	5	6
7	8	9	10	11	12	13
14	15	16	17	18	19	20
21	22	23	24	25	26	27
28	29	30	31			

¿Cuál es la fecha de hoy?
Es el primero de mayo.
  el dos de julio.
  el doce de octubre.
  17 - 3 - 95.

What is the date today?
  It's May first.
  July second.
  October 12.
  3 - 17 - 95.

abril
mayo
junio

octubre
noviembre
diciembre

enero
febrero
marzo

julio
agosto
septiembre

 Hoy por ti,
mañana por mí.

Every dog has his day.

Cuaderno de Nilda

Estudia para el examen de inglés:

1. tomorrow (mi cumpleaños)
2. the day after tomorrow
3. yesterday
4. the day before yesterday
5. the day
6. the holiday (¡Bravo!)
7. the school day
8. the birthday (mañana)
9. the week
10. the weekend (¡mi vida!)
11. the month

Nilda's Notebook

Study for English test:

1. mañana
2. pasado mañana
3. ayer
4. anteayer
5. el día
6. la fiesta
7. el día escolar
8. el cumpleaños
9. la semana
10. el fin de semana
11. el mes

Weekdays and Mythology

Derivations and Comparisons

Spanish Day	Roman Mythology
lunes	day honoring the moon god "luna" = moon
martes	day honoring the god of war, Mars
miércoles	day honoring Mercury, messenger of the gods
jueves	day honoring Jupiter or Jove, father and king of the gods
viernes	day honoring Venus, goddess of love
sábado	day honoring Saturn, god of the harvest and agriculture
domingo	day honoring "the Lord" "dominus" = the Lord Christian conversion of "solis dies" "solis dies" = day of the sun

Exercises

A Write in numerical form the dates your teacher reads.

1. _____

2. _____

3. _____

4. _____

5. _____

REMINDER: Where did you put the number for the day? _____

B Label the current month. Include the names of the days and all the numbers.

MES _____

DÍA	DÍA	DÍA	DÍA	DÍA	DÍA	DÍA

C Escribe las fechas.

1. Tuesday, April 1st _____

2. Wednesday, May 2nd _____

3. Thursday, September 16th _____

4. Friday, July 26th _____

5. Sunday, March 17th _____

D Asocia el inglés con el español.

1. hoy _____   a. yesterday

2. anteayer _____   b. the day after tomorrow

3. pasado mañana _____   c. today

4. ayer _____   d. tomorrow

5. mañana _____   e. the day before yesterday

E Escribe en español.

1. the first month of the year _____

2. the day that usually begins the school week _____

3. a windy month *en primavera* _____

4. the day on which Thanksgiving is celebrated _____

5. the month in which school ends _____

6. the last day of the week _____

7. the month of U.S. independence _____

8. the month in which Columbus Day is celebrated _____

9. the month in which *otōno* ends _____

10. the month in which Valentine's Day is celebrated _____

F Escribe el día en español, según el dibujo.

1. _____

2. _____

3. _____

4. _____

5. _____

6. _____

7. _____

G   Lee el párrafo. Escoge las respuestas correctas.

La corrida de toros es un famoso espectáculo español. Hay una corrida cada domingo. Hoy es domingo y es también el cumpleaños de Pepe. El asiste con su familia a la corrida en Málaga. Es su regalo de cumpleaños. El matador entra con su cuadrilla y marcha alrededor de la plaza de toros. La música comienza y todo el mundo grita, "¡Olé!" Con su traje de luces y sombrero de tres picos, el matador es una figura muy impresionante. Entra el toro y la corrida comienza. ¡Qué día más divertido!

> **la corrida de toros** = the bullfight
> **la plaza de toros** = the bullfighting stadium
> **cada** = each
> **el regalo** = the present
> **matador** = the bullfighter
> **la cuadrilla** = team of assistants
> **el pico** = the peak
> **divertido** = enjoyable
> **alrededor de** = around

1. Una diversión popular de España es. . . .
   - a. la plaza de toros
   - b. el béisbol
   - c. la corrida de toros
   - d. Pepe
2. Un grito típico de la corrida es. . .
   - a. ¡No más!
   - b. ¡Qué le vaya bien!
   - c. ¡Mátelo!
   - d. ¡Olé!
3. El matador lleva. . . .
   - a. un abrigo
   - b. un traje de luces
   - c. una sonrisa
   - d. un sombrero de jipijapa
4. Es el. . .de Pepe.
   - a. feria
   - b. toro
   - c. cumpleaños
   - d. padre
5. La corrida de toros es. . . .
   - a. en Málaga
   - b. en México
   - c. en Madrid
   - d. en La Habana

Crucigrama

H

Vertical

1. first full month of spring
2. month noted for its wind
3. harvest month
4. month named for Julius Caesar
6. month that begins the year
7. autumn month of thirty days
9. day before "domingo"
10. last month of the year
13. last day of the school week
15. Seven of these make a week.

Horizontal

2. month that "brings flowers"
4. Jove's day
5. last full month of winter
8. month that follows "mayo"
11. yesterday's tomorrow
12. month in which classes resume
14. precedes "martes"
16. "día...(*of school*)"
17. "enero," "mayo," "junio," etc.

Días Feriados Nacionales

Además de los siguientes días feriados, muchas ciudades y pueblos de Nicaragua también celebran sus propias festividades.

Enero 1	Día de Año Nuevo
Marzo o Abril	Jueves y Viernes Santos
Mayo 1	Día del Trabajo
Julio 19	Triunfo de la Revolución de 1979
Septiembre 14	Batalla de San Jacinto
Septiembre 15	Día de la Independencia
Noviembre 2	Día de los Fieles Difuntos
Diciembre 8	Inmaculada Concepción (Purísima)
Diciembre 25	Navidad

DURANTE LOS MESES DE VERANO, JULIO, AGOSTO Y SEPTIEMBRE, NO ABRIMOS LOS DOMINGOS

Cumpleaños feliz

27-03-73	27-03-74	28-03-66	30-03-72	30-03-74
Imanol Etxeberria Portero del Athletic.	**Gaizka Mendieta** Defensa del Valencia.	**Frank Passi** Centrocampista del Compostela.	**Harold Lozano** Centrocampista del Valladolid.	**Igor Gluscevic** Delantero del Extremadura.

MARZO

1

L	M	M	J	V	S	D
				1	2	3
4	5	6	7	8	9	10
11	12	13	14	15	16	17
18	19	20	21	22	23	24
25	26	27	28	29	30	31

VIERNES

LITERATURE
La literatura

Five Great Authors

Miguel de Cervantes, the author of Spain's most beloved novel, *Don Quijote de la Mancha*, was born in Alcalá de Henares in 1547. He lived a life almost as unbelievable as that of his famous character. Cervantes was a wanderer, a soldier, a prisoner of pirates, a disgraced public official, a mediocre poet and dramatist, and finally, Spain's most famous novelist. Fighting against the Turks, he lost the use of his left hand at the battle of Lepanto. While returning to Spain from this battle, he was captured by pirates who made him a prisoner and sent him to the galleys. Five years later Cervantes escaped from his captors and returned home. Upon arriving, he was appointed mayor of his town. Later, when money was found missing from the town's account, he spent time in jail. He left in disgrace after his release. Cervantes tried writing both poems and plays with little success. He also wrote novels. In 1615 he published *Don Quijote de la Mancha*, which was an immediate success and led to great honor. His *Novelas ejemplares*, twelve short novels, are still considered masterpieces of Spanish prose. Cervantes died in 1616.

Don Quijote de la Mancha is a satirical novel about a nobleman, don Quijote. The hero is driven mad by his excessive reading of novels of chivalry. Full of noble ideals, don Quijote sets out in quest of good deeds to perform, fair maidens to rescue, and vicious dragons to slay. Accompanied by his squire, Sancho Panza, he has many misadventures that are quite humorous to the reader and quite unpleasant for the hero. Don Quijote is finally sobered by the results of his misadventures and vows never to read such stories again. The modern musical, *Man of la Mancha*, is based on this famous work.

Gustavo Adolfo Bécquer (1836–70) was one of Spain's great romantic poets. He was born in Seville but moved to Madrid at the age of eighteen. It was there, in the capital, that this young poet hoped to achieve literary fame. However, both he and his brother Valeriano, an artist, earned only a meager living writing verse and selling paintings. It was said that both brothers existed more on ideals than on nourishment. They died in poverty in 1870.

Quien bien anda, bien acaba.   All's well that ends well.

Bécquer's most famous poems are found in the collection *Rimas*, published in 1871. These poems are considered models of romantic verse. Bécquer's poetry is personal, sentimental, free, rebellious, and wild. Its themes are escape, piracy, love, and idealism. His verse is very musical and creates feelings of happiness and sympathy. Students of Spanish literature study this poetry seriously.

Rubén Darío was the pen name of Félix Rubén García Saramiento, one of Latin America's greatest lyric poets. Born in Melapa, Nicaragua, Darío displayed a talent for writing and pursued a career in journalism. He obtained a job as a reporter for *La Nación*, Argentina's most respected newspaper. As its foreign bureau chief, Darío traveled to Chile, France, Spain, and Italy. He quickly mastered French and Italian and made friends with the poets of these lands. Darío was greatly influenced by the French poets. In 1904 he was appointed diplomatic minister to Brazil. He held a similar post in Spain from 1908 to 1911. Darío was recognized for his poetic talent and lectured on poetry and the arts in Europe, South America, and the United States. He was greatly concerned with the freedom of his tiny republic and quite upset with the role of the United States in the internal affairs of Nicaragua. He voiced his concerns in a poem entitled *Oda a Roosevelt*. Many of Darío's poems have patriotic themes. He died of pneumonia in 1916.

Darío's poetry was "New World" in style. He employed in a modern manner all he had learned from the classical writers and the modern poets of Europe. His poems greatly influenced future writers of Spanish poetry. He published his first book of poems, *Azul*, in 1888, and the critics praised it highly. *Cantos de vida y esperanza* and *Prosas profanas* were published next. This outstanding poet blended ideas with color and electrifying sound. To honor his artistic achievement, his country has renamed Melapa. It is now Ciudad Darío.

Emilia Bazán (1852-1921) is known as one of Spain's outstanding novelists. Bazán was a countess, the only daughter of Count Pardo Bazán. She was a child prodigy and could read and write well by age four. Historical practices and traditions had made it difficult for most women to be well educated, but changes in the late nineteenth and early twentieth centuries provided increased opportunities for women authors. Bazán took advantage of the opportunities. By age fourteen she was writing scholarly commentaries on the *Bible*, the *Iliad*, the *Divine Comedy*, and other great works.

Bazán introduced "naturalism" into her novels. Naturalism views human beings as part of nature. Each person is, therefore, subject to nature's two great forces, heredity and environment. The people in Bazán's novels struggle with these forces.

Bazán loved her native province of Galicia and spent her summer there every year. Her novels use Galicia for their setting and are models of fine description, skillful plots, and understanding of people. *Los pazos de Ulloa* and *La madre naturaleza* are her two finest novels. The author was prominent in the cause of women's rights and chaired the Department for Literature at the University of Madrid.

Carmen Laforet (1921-) was born in Barcelona. Her father was an outgoing athlete and sportsman who excelled in cycling and shooting. He was also a successful architect. Her mother was religious, caring, and gentle. Laforet seemed to inherit all of her parents' good qualities. She was only thirteen when her mother died, which grieved her greatly. The coldness of her stepmother did little to lighten her sorrow.

After high school Laforet studied first the liberal arts and then law at the university. She abandoned her studies, however, and turned to writing. She was immediately successful. In 1944, at 23, she published her novel, *Nada.* It won Spain's highest honor for the novel, the *Premio Eugenio Nadal. La isla y los demonios,* published in 1952, confirmed her outstanding literary skill. Her novel *La mujer nueva* won the *Premio Menorca* in 1955 and the *Premio Miguel de Cervantes* in 1956.

The author introduced "spiritualism" into the novel. Spiritualism is a theory that sees people as more than material beings. According to this theory, a human being must respect nature but look for total happiness beyond material things. In the novel *Nada,* Andrea, the main character, is deeply moved by the meaningless lives of those about her. She comes away from her experiences more understanding, more serious, and ready to look beyond the material for solutions to life's problems.

Exercises

A Guess who...

1. was a galley slave. _____

2. wrote about pirates. _____

3. was a child prodigy. _____

4. was a reporter. _____

5. was born in Nicaragua. _____

6. was injured in the battle of Lepanto. _____

7. studied the arts and law. _____

B Asocia el inglés con el español.

	A		**B**
1.	Sancho Panza _____	a.	Latin American poet
2.	Bécquer _____	b.	Spain's greatest author
3.	Rubén Darío _____	c.	poems by Bécquer
4.	Cervantes _____	d.	a poet who died young
5.	*Rimas* _____	e.	a character created by Cervantes

C Write the full name of the author of each work listed below.

1. *Nada* _____

2. *Azul* _____

3. *Rimas* _____

4. *Don Quijote de la Mancha* _____

5. *Prosas profanas* _____

6. *Novelas ejemplares* _____

7. *La madre naturaleza* _____

D Complete the analogies.

1. _____ : novel = Bécquer: poem

2. Cervantes: chivalry = _____ : piracy

3. Darío: _____ = Bécquer: Spain

4. Rubén: Darío = Miguel : _____

5. satire: _____ = patriotism: Darío

6. naturalism: Bazán = spiritualism: _____

E ¿Qué nombre corresponde a cada dibujo?

Cervantes

Darío

Bécquer

F Which writer would most likely...

1. be an expert on art? _____

2. guide friends through Galicia? _____

3. prefer to travel only on land? _____

4. discuss poetry at a French café? _____

5. appreciate fine architecture? _____

6. laugh at himself? _____

7. object strenuously if a foreign country were to take advantage of his people?

_____

G Label each plot described below as classical, modern, or romantic.

1. Paco Ramírez decides to avenge himself against an unjust government that stole his farm. He enlists a band of rebels and flees to the mountains to plan a revolution.

_____

2. Doña Elvira decides to abandon her plans to marry don Franco whom she greatly loves. Her decision springs from her sense of familial duty, which requires her to remain at home to care for her aged parents.

_____

3. In the lyric "The Orange-Smelling Field," the one-eyed leaf spies on the purple odor who lives in the grove of white water vapors. All is reported to Doctor Colorsmell.

_____

H Completa las frases.

1. _____ was a poet who lived in dire poverty.

2. _____'s birthplace was renamed for him.

3. _____ and _____were two

    great poets.

4. _____ was a great novelist.

5. _____, _____,

    _____ and _____ were all

    from Spain.

6. _____ was from Latin America.

7. _____ had a brother who was an artist.

8. _____ served as mayor of his town.

9. _____ represented his nation in Europe.

10. _____ was a wounded war hero.

RINCONETE Y CORTADILLO
MIGUEL DE CERVANTES

¡ADIÓS, PAPÁ!
ÓSCAR TOSAL

LA CORZA BLANCA
GUSTAVO ADOLFO BÉCQUER

LA CIUDAD DE LOS DIOSES
LUIS Mª CARRERO PÉREZ

EL MISTERIO DE LA LLAVE
ELENA MORENO

Jorge Luis Borges
El Aleph

Jorge Luis Borges
Obras completas
1975
1985

Jorge Luis Borges
Obras completas
1960
1972

Jorge Luis Borges
Obras completas
1940
1960

Jorge Luis Borges
Obras completas
1923
1936

EN EL REY, PRIMERA BIOGRAFÍA ÑOL NARRA SU EVOLUCIÓN PARA SER EDUCADO BAJO HASTA EL HOMBRE DE ESTADO JUAN CARLOS I DE ESPAÑA PORTANTES DE SU VIDA COMO DE LA CORONA -D.JUAN DE BORBÓN-, DE REY" DE FRANCISCO FRANCO, Y CIPALES ARTÍFICES DE LA TRANSICIÓN AUTORIZADA, EL PROPIO MONARCA ESPA- DESDE EL NIÑO ENVIADO POR SU PADRE, LA TUTELA DEL GENERAL FRANCO, QUE FRUSTRÓ EL GOLPE DEL 23-F. EVOCA LOS MOMENTOS MÁS IM- HIJO DEL HEREDERO LEGÍTIMO COMO SUCESOR "A TÍTULO COMO UNO DE LOS PRIN- POLÍTICA ESPAÑOLA.

José Luis de Vilallonga
EL REY
D. JUAN CARLOS I DE ESPAÑA
PLAZA & JANÉS

PLAZA & JANES

© Cambio 16

Ana María Matute ha revisado a fondo esta novela, escrita hace cuarenta años.

Ana María Matute
Luciérnagas
CÍRCULO DE LECTORES

En vísperas de la guerra civil, Sol, una adolescente de la alta burguesía barcelonesa, vive su existencia de privilegios: inviernos en prestigiosos colegios, veranos en la costa... La feliz rutina se interrumpe el día en que su padre, un próspero industrial, es asesinado, víctima del odio desatado por los acontecimientos. Vendrá entonces el frío, el hambre, el miedo, y Sol pasa de los sueños infantiles al amargo despertar de la realidad para convertirse en mujer. Ana María Matute dibuja con maestría el desquiciado mundo de la guerra y el atónito descubrimiento del primer amor.

NUEVO
Ana María Matute
LUCIÉRNAGAS
13 × 21 cm. 320 páginas. Géltex color con estampaciones. Sobrecubierta plastificada. Guardas color.

el otoño del patriarca
Gabriel García Márquez

Mario Vargas Llosa
PANTALEÓN Y LAS VISITADORAS

obras completas de ALEJO CARPENTIER
II
el reino de este mundo y los pasos perdidos

Gabriel García Márquez
Cien años de soledad
Edición de Jacques Joset
CÁTEDRA
Letras Hispánicas

CIEN AÑOS DE SOLEDAD
Gabriel García Márquez
4¼" x 7" - 493 pgs.
Cód. 104 - Reg. $10.50

Ganadora del Premio Nobel, es la obra máxima de la literatura hispanoamericana.

LEISURE AND RECREATION
El tiempo libre y las diversiones

¿Adónde vas tú?
Where are you going?

Voy al partido.
I'm going to the game.

Voy al museo.
I'm going to the museum.

Voy a la fiesta.
I'm going to the party.

Voy a la playa.
I'm going to the beach.

Marcos:	¿Adónde vas tú esta noche?	Where are you going tonight?
Tomás:	Voy al partido.	I'm going to the game.
Marcos:	¡Yo también!	Me, too!

❀❀❀❀❀

Andrés:	¿Adónde vas tú hoy?	Where are you going today?
Patricia:	Voy al museo...al Museo del Prado.*	I'm going to the museum...to the Prado Museum.
Andrés:	¿Por qué?	Why?
Patricia:	Para ver la exhibición de Goya.	To see the Goya exhibit.

* *The Prado, Spain's most prominent art museum, is located in Madrid.*

En la variedad está el gusto.   Variety is the spice of life.

Juego al volibol.
I play volleyball.

Juego al fútbol.
I play soccer.

¿ Qué deportes haces tú ?
What sports do you play ?

Juego al tenis.
I play tennis.

Juego al básquetbol.
I play basketball.

Juego al béisbol.
I play baseball.

¿Qué te gusta hacer?
What do you like to do?

Me gusta esquiar.
I like skiing.

Me gusta montar a caballo.
I like horseback riding.

Me gusta leer.
I like reading.

Me gusta bailar.
I like dancing.

Me gusta nadar.
I like swimming.

Me gusta montar en bicicleta.
I like biking.

Susana:	Mañana hay un picnic.		There's a picnic tomorrow.
Juanita:	¿Dónde?		Where?
Susana:	En la playa. ¿Quieres ir conmigo?		At the beach. Do you want to go with me?
Juanita:	Sí. Me encanta nadar.		Yes. I love swimming.

Lucía:	¿Vas a la fiesta esta noche?		Are you going to the party tonight?
Daniel:	Claro. Va a haber música, ¿verdad?		Of course. There'll be music, won't there?
Lucía:	Sí. Me encanta bailar.		Yes. I love dancing.

A ¿Adónde vas tú? Completa cada frase en español.

1. Voy al _____ . (*game*)

2. Voy a un _____ . (*picnic*)

3. Voy a la _____ . (*party*)

4. Voy al _____ . (*museum*)

5. Voy a la _____ . (*beach*)

B Select the correct answers based on the previous dialogues.

1. ¿Cuándo es el partido?
   a. mañana   b. viernes
   c. esta noche   d. a las ocho

2. ¿Qué es el Prado?
   a. un caballo   b. un partido
   c. una exhibición de Goya   d. un museo

3. ¿Quién es Goya?
   a. un profesor   b. un pintor
   c. un museo   d. un actor

4. ¿Cuándo es el picnic?
   a. mañana   b. hoy
   c. en la playa   d. yo también

5. ¿Dónde es el picnic?
   a. a la fiesta   b. al Prado
   c. al béisbol   d. en la playa

C ¿Qué deportes haces tú? Completa cada frase en español.

1. Juego al _____ .

2. Juego al _____ .

3. Juego al _____ .

4. Juego al _____ .

5. Juego al _____ .

D Descifra las palabras.

1. TARDIOP _____

2. CPIINC _____

3. YPLAA _____

4. SAIFET _____

5. USOME _____

E ¿Qué te gusta hacer? Completa cada frase en español.

1. Me gusta _____.

2. Me gusta _____.

3. Me gusta _____.

4. Me gusta _____ .

5. Me gusta _____ .

6. Me gusta _____ .

F Completa el diálogo en español.

Mónica: ¿Adónde _____ tú hoy?

Patricia: Voy _____ la playa. ¿Quieres _____ conmigo?

Mónica: _____ . Me encanta el océano.

Patricia: ¿Qué _____ haces tú en la playa?

Mónica: Me gusta _____ en el océano y

_____ al volibol.

G Lee el párrafo. Escoge las respuestas correctas.

Dolores organiza una fiesta pequeña en la playa. Ella invita a sus amigos Yolanda, Felipe, Juan Carlos, Rosario y Guillermo a la fiesta. La fiesta comienza a las tres. Hace buen tiempo hoy porque hace calor y no está nublado. A los amigos les gusta nadar en el océano y jugar al volibol. Después de las actividades, va a haber un picnic con sandwiches de jamón y de pollo, salchichas, bebidas y helados. ¡La fiesta en la playa va a ser magnífica!

> **les gusta** = (they) like
> **después de** = after
> **va a ser** = is going to be

1. ¿Quién va a la fiesta de Dolores?
   a. sus padres
   c. sus hermanas
   b. sus amigos
   d. sus tíos

2. ¿A qué hora comienza la fiesta?
   a. a la playa
   c. a las tres
   b. a medianoche
   d. a las doce menos diez

3. ¿Qué tiempo hace?
   a. Hace buen tiempo.
   c. Nieva.
   b. Llueve.
   d. Hace frío.

4. ¿Qué les gusta a los amigos?
   a. Les gusta bailar.
   c. Les gusta nadar y jugar al volibol.
   b. Les gusta jugar al fútbol.
   d. Les gusta montar a caballo.

5. ¿Qué comida va a haber en el picnic?
   a. una playa
   c. unos sandwiches
   b. un restaurante
   d. un vaso

REPÚBLICA DOMINICANA

SAMMY SOSA

PEDRO MARTÍNEZ

MULTICINES

POSIBILIDADES DE PROGRAMACIÓN

Cine	★ Estrenos	CA Clásicos	Temáticos	
TV	Series. Temáticos	Infantiles y familiares	Documentales	
Música	Varios	Clásica	Radio	
Noticias	Actualidad	Internacional		
Canales	Guía de programación	Deportes	Temáticos	

SERVICIOS AVANZADOS

A corto plazo permitirá accesos a Internet, videojuegos, servicio telebanco, telecompra, prensa electrónica, teleeducación, encuestas...

Vivan las VACACIONES

TEATRO CAMPOAMOR

Teatro en Enero

José Ordóñez

21 y 22 de Enero
Compañía Teatro de La Abadía
"Entremeses". Miguel de Cervantes
Sesión 20:00 horas
Grupos de Estudiantes y Universitarios precios especiales
Localidades a la venta

Comunidad de Madrid
CAJA DE ASTURIAS
Fundación de Cultura
AYUNTAMIENTO DE OVIEDO

PARQUE
PLAZA SESAMO

MONTERREY, MEXICO

CLUB PRIVADO

CURSOS DE NATACION, TENIS, PATINAJE, TAEKWONDO

- Cursos vacaciones
- Matronatación y estimulación temprana
- Programas para colegios y jardines infantiles
- Planes y horarios especiales para ejecutivos

12o. FESTIVAL INTERNACIONAL

TEATRO

MANIZALES
COLOMBIA 7 AL 14 DE SEPTIEMBRE
Banco Cafetero

EL REGLAMENTO DICTA SENTENCIA

El trío arbitral es "aire" sobre el terreno de juego. Ante cualquier duda el Reglamento dicta sentencia.

En la ilustración observamos cómo rebota el balón en el árbitro y entra en la portería. El gol es válido y debe concederse.

SHOPPING
Las compras

Yo hago mis compras...
I shop...

el vendedor
salesclerk

la clienta
customer

los tenis
athletic shoes

...en el centro comercial.
...at the shopping center (mall).

Ana:	¿Adónde vas tú?	Where are you going?
Federico:	Al centro comercial.	To the shopping center.
Ana:	¿Qué vas a comprar?	What are you going to buy?
Federico:	Unos tenis.	Some athletic shoes.

❀❀❀❀❀

Vendedor:	Buenos días, señora. ¿En qué puedo servirle?	Hello, Ma'am. May I help you?
Clienta:	Estoy mirando, nada más. Gracias.	I'm just looking. Thanks.

 Al que llegue primero, se le sirve primero. First come, first served.

Cliente:	¿Cuánto cuesta este CD?	How much is this CD?
Cajera:	Cuesta 28,00 pesos.	It costs 28 pesos.
Cliente:	¡Es un poco caro!	That's a little expensive!
Cajera:	No, es barato.	No, it's cheap.
Cliente:	Está bien. Lo compro. Aquí está el dinero, señorita.	OK. I'll buy it. Here's the money, Miss.
Cajera:	Muchas gracias. Aquí está el cambio.	Thank you very much. Here's your change.

| Vendedora: | ¿Algo más? | Anything else? |
| Cliente: | Pues, tres tomates, cinco duraznos y unas habichuelas. Sí, eso es todo. | Uhm...three tomatoes, five peaches and some green beans. Yes, that's all. |

Exercises

A Asocia la columna **A** con la columna **B**.

A

1. tenis _____
2. habichuelas _____
3. CD _____
4. silla _____
5. bolígrafos y cuadernos _____

B

a. market
b. shoe store
c. furniture store
d. stationery store
e. music store

B Completa cada frase en español, según la ilustración.

1. Me encantan los _____ .

2. La señora Blanca escoje unas frutas buenas en

   el _____ .

3. Hago mis compras en el

   _____ .

4. Aquí está el _____ ,
   señor.

5. El CD es barato. _____
   19,00 pesos.

C Choose the expression from the following list that completes each sentence correctly.

barato   pesos   comprar

caja   compras

Alicia hace sus _____ en la tienda. Ella va a

_____ un CD de música clásica. Este CD cuesta

21,00 _____ . No es caro. Es

_____ . Ella va a la

_____ con su CD.

D Contesta las preguntas en español.

1. If you see the sign "Ofertas," how would you expect the price of the object to be?
   - a. barato
   - b. el dinero
   - c. caro
   - d. la moneda

2. What do you reply if the cashier says "Cuesta 40,00 pesos"?
   - a. Aquí está el dinero.
   - b. ¿Dónde está la tienda?
   - c. ¿Cuánto cuesta?
   - d. Gracias, eso es todo.

3. What do you get back if you give the cashier too much money?
   - a. la caja
   - b. el cambio
   - c. barato
   - d. unas habichuelas

4. Who helps you find what you need?
   - a. el dinero
   - b. el vendedor
   - c. la cajera
   - d. la clienta

5. What do you say if you don't need the salesclerk's help right now?
   - a. ¿En qué puedo servirle?
   - b. ¡Es un poco caro!
   - c. Estoy mirando, nada más.
   - d. ¿Algo más?

E Escoje la respuesta correcta.

1. ¿Eso es todo?
   - a. No, es caro.
   - b. No, pues, unos duraznos, por favor.
   - c. No, es barato.
   - d. No, estoy mirando, nada más.

2. ¿Por qué vas tú a la tienda?
   - a. No tengo sed.
   - b. Llevo una bata.
   - c. Hay un picnic.
   - d. Yo hago mis compras.

3. ¿Son baratos los tenis?
   - a. Sí, aquí está el cambio.
   - b. No, es el vendedor.
   - c. No, son caros.
   - d. Sí, eso es todo.

4. ¿Cuánto cuesta el CD?
   - a. Cuesta 24,00 pesos.
   - b. Pues, estoy mirando, nada más.
   - c. Eso es todo.
   - d. En el centro comercial.

5. ¿Qué vas a comprar?
   - a. ofertas
   - b. un vendedor
   - c. unos tomates y unas habichuelas
   - d. el cambio

F Tomás is shopping in a clothing store. Complete his conversation with the salesclerk.

Vendedor: Buenos días, señor. ¿En qué puedo

_____?

Tomás: Estoy _____ , nada más. Gracias.

Vendedor: Hay muchas ofertas. Todo está _____ :

las camisas, los pantalones, los abrigos y los zapatos.

Tomás: Gracias, señor. Pues, ¿ _____ cuesta este

pantalón negro?

Vendedor: _____ 70,00 pesos. Es barato, ¿verdad?

Tomás: No, es un poco _____ . No puedo

_____ el pantalón. Tengo 35,00 pesos,

_____ más.

Crucigrama

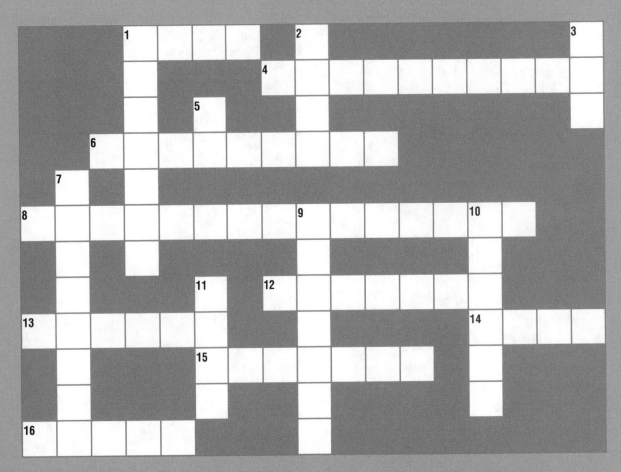

G

Vertical

1. a female customer
2. the opposite of "barato"
3. "¿Algo...?"
5. compact disc
7. "¿En qué puedo...?"
9. where you buy fresh vegetables
10. "¿...vas tú?"
11. "Eso es...." (all)

Horizontal

1. a cash register
4. a long, thin, green vegetable
6. a female salesclerk
8. a shopping center
12. "Al que llegue..., se le sirve primero."
13. what you pay your bill with
14. "Estoy mirando,...más."
15. fruit that has a fuzzy exterior
16. sporty "zapatos"

Fans
SI ES MODA

ROPA JUVENIL
De venta en los mejores almacenes del país

Información
del contenido comercial
de nuestras Tiendas

El Corte Inglés

OVIEDO
URÍA

4 INFANTIL. Moda y Zapatería. BEBÉS. JUGUETES. CAFETERÍA-RESTAURANTE.

3 JÓVENES. Moda y Zapatería. Territorio Vaquero. Primeras marcas. Tiendas de Moda. Punto de Información Universitaria.

2 HOMBRE. Moda y Zapatería. Marcas exclusivas. Complementos. Firmas Internacionales. Sastrería a Medida. Peluquería de Hombre. Club del Gourmet. VIAJES EL CORTE INGLÉS. CENTRO DE SEGUROS.

1 MUJER. Moda y Zapatería. Marcas Exclusivas. Firmas Internacionales. Lencería y Corsetería. Punto. Peletería. Novias. Peluquería de Mujer.

B COMPLEMENTOS DE MODA. Cosmética y Perfumería. Joyería. Bisutería. Relojería. Óptica. ARTÍCULOS PARA FUMADOR Y SOUVENIRS. PAPELERÍA. FOTOGRAFÍA.

DEPORTES. Moda y Zapatería. Grandes Marcas. Tienda Aventura. DISCOS Y LIBROS. LISTAS DE BODA. CARTA DE COMPRAS. SERVICIO DE ATENCIÓN AL CLIENTE.

S1

S2 APARCAMIENTO.

S3 APARCAMIENTO.

Alimentación

ACEITE DE ORUJO
Y OLIVA **MIL OLIVAS**
GARRAFA 2 LITROS
sale el litro a 448

895

HARINA
OROMAS
PQTE. KILO

75

PASTAS DE SOPA
OROMAS
PAQUETE 500 GRS.

69

CENTRO COMERCIAL
HACIENDA SANTA BARBARA

Carrera 7a. con Avenida Pepe Sierra.

Brillamos... porque tenemos **luz** propia.

Compras, Restaurantes,
Entretenimiento,
Lo que *Quiera.*

¡NO te lo pierdas!

≡ **Kukulcán**
Plaza

Blvd. Kukulcán km 13 ✷ Zona Hotelera ✷ Cancún, Q. Roo. México ✷ Tel: (98) 85.22.00
e-mail: kukulcan@cancun.novenet.com.mx

¡COMPRE
LO QUE QUIERA
CON SOLO
MOVER
UN DEDO!

PAGAR CON LA RED SI PAGA !

RED MULTICOLOR

TRAVEL AND TRANSPORTATION
Los viajes y los medios de transporte

¿Cómo viajas tú?

How do you travel?

Yo viajo en avión.
I travel by plane.

Yo viajo en autobús.
I travel by bus.

Yo viajo en carro.
I travel by car.

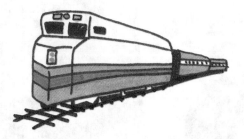

Yo viajo en tren.
I travel by train.

Yo viajo en barco.
I travel by ship.

 Viajando se instruye la gente. Whoever travels far knows much.

en el aeropuerto
at the airport

la empleada
clerk

el pasaporte
passport

la maleta
suitcase

el mostrador
ticket counter

el viajero
traveler

Empleada:	¿Su pasaporte, señor?	Your passport, Sir?
Viajero:	Está en mi maleta, señorita.	It's in my suitcase, Miss.
Empleada:	Pero Ud. debe tenerlo consigo...y especialmente en el control de pasaportes, al llegar.	But you must have it on you...and especially at passport control upon arrival.
Viajero:	De acuerdo. Espere Ud..... ¿Y dónde abordamos nosotros?	OK. Wait.... And where do we board?
Empleada:	En la puerta 20, a la derecha.	At gate 20, on your right.

Viajera:	Señor, ¿a qué hora sale el siguiente tren para Madrid?	What time does the next train for Madrid leave, Sir?
Empleado:	Al mediodía, señora. Aquí está el horario.	At noon, Ma'am. Here's the schedule.
Viajera:	Bueno, pues, me gustaría comprar un boleto de ida y vuelta de segunda clase.	Good, then I'd like a round-trip ticket in second class.
Empleado:	Aquí está el boleto. Son 41 euros.	Here's the ticket. It's 41 euro.

| Sr. León: | Señora...¿cómo puedo llegar al hotel Ritz? | Ma'am...how do I get to the Ritz Hotel? |
| Sra. Jurado: | Tome Ud. el autobús número 2 y bájese Ud. en la oficina de correos. El hotel está a la izquierda. | Take bus number 2 and get off at the post office. The hotel is on the left. |

Ejercicios

A Match the English with the Spanish.

1. Espere Ud. _____
2. me gustaría _____
3. a la izquierda _____
4. Bájese en la oficina _____
   de correos.
5. ¿Dónde abordamos? _____
6. Tome Ud. el autobús. _____
7. un boleto de ida y vuelta _____
8. Ud. debe tenerlo consigo. _____
9. Aquí está el horario. _____
10. a la derecha _____

a. a round-trip ticket

b. on the right

c. Where do we board?

d. Here's the schedule.

e. Get off at the post office.

f. You must have it on you.

g. Wait.

h. I would like

i. Take the bus.

j. on the left

B ¿Cómo viajas tú? Completa cada frase en español.

1. Yo viajo _____ .

2. Yo viajo _____ .

3. Yo viajo _____ .

4. Yo viajo _____ .

5. Yo viajo _____ .

C Contesta las preguntas en español.

1. Where do you go to take a train?
   a. al aeropuerto
   b. en el control de pasaportes
   c. a la estación del tren
   d. en la calle

2. What do you ask if you want directions to the train station?
   a. ¿Y dónde abordamos?
   b. ¿Cómo puedo llegar a la estación del tren?
   c. ¿A qué hora sale el tren?
   d. ¿En qué puedo servirle?

3. What would you look at to find the times when trains, buses, planes, etc. arrive and leave?
   a. el horario
   b. el mostrador
   c. el pasaporte
   d. la maleta

4. What would you say if you wanted to buy a ticket?
   a. Aquí está mi pasaporte.
   b. Me gustaría comprar un boleto.
   c. ¿Adónde vas tú?
   d. ¿Cómo puedo llegar a la oficina de correos?

5. If you don't want a first-class ticket, what do you say?
   a. un boleto de ida y vuelta
   b. un boleto
   c. el autobús número 2
   d. de segunda

D Decifra las palabras.

1. ATSRROMDO _____

2. ROHIRAO _____

3. ORNCOLT ED STEPRAASOP

   _____

4. JOVERIA _____

5. PRATOSPAE _____

E Lee el párrafo. Escoje las respuestas correctas.

Hace buen tiempo hoy. Adán y Patricio están en la estación del tren. Van a viajar en tren. Adán va a comprar dos boletos para ir a Barcelona. Los abuelos de Adán viven cerca de Barcelona. Los dos amigos esperan el tren en el andén número 4. El tren llega a la estación a las catorce horas. Cuando llega, ellos abordan el tren. Adán escoge un asiento cerca de la ventana. Los amigos hablan de su visita a Barcelona donde hay mucho que hacer. Están felices. Al llegar, toman el autobús para ir a la casa de los abuelos de Adán.

> **cerca de** = near
> **esperan** = they wait for
> **andén** = platform
> **llega** = arrives
> **asiento** = seat

1. ¿Dónde están Adán y Patricio?
   a. en el aeropuerto
   c. en el taxi
   b. en el autobús
   d. en la estación del tren

2. ¿Adónde viajan Adán y Patricio hoy?
   a. a Sevilla
   c. a Córdoba
   b. a Barcelona
   d. a Santiago

3. ¿Cuántos boletos compra Adán?
   a. dos
   c. catorce
   b. uno
   d. cuatro

4. ¿Dónde esperan el tren?
   a. cerca de la ventana
   c. en el andén número 4
   b. en el mostrador
   d. en las maletas

5. ¿Cómo van ellos a la casa de los abuelos de Adán?
   a. en avión
   c. en carro
   b. en autobús
   d. en barco

F Complete the analogies.

1. empleado: _____ = viajero: viajera

2. avión: aeropuerto = tren: _____

3. barco: océano = autobús: _____

4. empleado: _____ = profesor: escritorio

5. uno: dos = primero: _____